PRAISE FOR
The Big Ten of Grammar

"I have not found computerized grammar checks to be very reliable, nor have I seen a convenient grammar reference source in my twenty-five years of legal practice. *The Big Ten of Grammar* is a quick way to check one's recollection of hard-to-remember grammar rules. Dr. Bradshaw includes great examples for each rule and a brief but comprehensive recap at the end of each chapter. *The Big Ten of Grammar* is my new favorite reference book."

— JANE COHEN, ATTORNEY AT LAW, ST. LOUIS, MISSOURI

"I thought I would never need a grammar book again after college, but I could not have been more wrong. Working in a top-level government office in Washington, I learned that a solid grasp of grammar is necessary to be considered credible. Dr. Bradshaw explains daily grammar in a clear and detailed fashion. I am now in graduate school, and *The Big Ten of Grammar* is my constant companion. It's a must for every serious student."

— NICOLE NORD, SAN FRANCISCO, CALIFORNIA

"With *The Big Ten of Grammar*, Dr. Bradshaw has not only identified the most frequent grammatical landmines, he has provided easy-to-remember techniques for avoiding them. It is a reference book I can carry in my head."

— CHARLIE CLAGGETT, VP MARKETING, WARSON BRANDS, ST. LOUIS, MISSOURI

"*The Big Ten of Grammar* is my compact resource for resolving pesky grammatical questions that plague most of us everyday. I teach a university Managerial Economics Class, which includes two writing assignments, and *The Big Ten of Grammar* will be a helpful resource for students."

— JOHN H. ARMSTRONG, BANKING PROFESSION~~~ S~ L~~~~ M~~~~~~I

"*The Big Ten of Grammar* is the m~~~~~~~~~~~~~~~~~~~~~~~~en
since *The One Min*~~~~~~~

— DAVE BUCK, MBA, NEW PRODU~~~~~~~~~~~~~~RI

"*The Big Ten of Grammar* is now my primary grammar reference and constant companion. Technology professionals are notoriously poor spellers and writers, so Dr. Bradshaw's straightforward guidelines are extremely useful in my work as a software development professional. Clear and precise software design documents are necessary to eliminate costly errors due to misinterpretation. Correct grammar is clearly a key ingredient for my work. Thank you, Dr. Bradshaw, for writing this book."

– Megan Mori, Principal, Mori Partners, Santa Barbara, California

"At first I hesitated to read *The Big Ten of Grammar*, thinking I knew it all, but after the second chapter I realized I had forgotten many of the rules of grammar. Thank you, Dr. Bradshaw, for reminding me of them in such a fun, memorable way. It is a great book I keep on my coffee table where I can reference it easily."

– G. Vietor Davis, Jr., Investments and former Real Estate Developments, Williamsburg, Virginia

"Engineers focus on technology with little time for proper grammar. Dr. Bradshaw's *The Big Ten of Grammar* makes a fine companion to spell-checking software, online dictionaries, and search engines. *The Big Ten of Grammar* brings precision and accuracy to professional writing."

– Larry Green, Internet Engineer, Southern California

"I love *The Big Ten of Grammar*! Correct grammar is easily forgotten as we age, but I find all of Dr. Bradshaw's examples especially helpful. *The Big Ten of Grammar* will make a wonderful reference book for my work. And my mother bought a copy for each of her seven college-age grandchildren."

– Sherry Struckhoff, RN, BSN, Health Science Instructor, Waynesville Career Center, Missouri

"Because of its clear and engaging explanations, *The Big Ten of Grammar* was an instant hit with teachers and secretaries in Parkway. Thank you, Dr. Bradshaw, for helping to curtail some of the most common grammar demons in workplace communication and student writing."

– Rebecca Langrall, EdD, Curriculum Coordinator, Secondary Communication Arts, Parkway School District

The Big Ten

of Grammar

The Big Ten

of Grammar

Identifying and Fixing
the Ten Most
Frequent Grammatical Errors

William B. Bradshaw, PhD

**BEAUFORT
BOOKS**

Cataloging-in-Publication Data available upon request.

LCCN: 2010923488
ISBN: 978-0-8253-0677-8
Hardcover ISBN: 978-0-9842-3585-8

For inquiries about volume orders, please contact:

Beaufort Books
27 West 20th Street, Suite 1102
New York, NY 10011
sales@beaufortbooks.com

Published in the United States by Beaufort Books
www.beaufortbooks.com

Distributed by Midpoint Trade Books
www.midpointtrade.com

Printed in the United States of America

To Mrs. Jones

and to all of the other teachers on various levels of education
who have gone beyond the call of duty in helping struggling
students to understand and achieve but who seldom get appropriately
thanked or recognized for their extra time and effort

Contents

Preface

During most of my professional career, I worked with not-for-profit institutions in various parts of the country. Regardless of where I was located—no matter the state or the setting—I found that the people I encountered all had something in common. From the highest authority to the youngest student, from the hotshot financier to the working-class parent, I found that they all had one thing in common: they all tended to make the same grammatical errors.

When I retired from a formal position that required my going to the office each day, I began a systematic study of the typical grammatical errors people make. I read newspapers, those from small towns that are known primarily to regional readers and some of the biggies with national and international audiences; I read professional journals from religious, educational, and philanthropic publishers; I listened to radio newscasters and watched the TV news from the major, cable, and satellite networks; I watched movies—old ones and new ones; I patiently listened to and watched commercials on radio and TV; I paid attention to highway billboards; I listened to the speeches of politicians and read their newsletters; I even resorted to watching soap operas. Again and again, I found the same grammatical errors. These findings led me to write *The Big Ten of Grammar: Identifying and*

Fixing the Ten Most Frequent Grammatical Errors.

When the book was first published in hardback, I developed a website: www.bigtenofgrammar.com. In the website I offered to answer grammatical questions and provided a way for readers to e-mail their questions to me. I received queries not only from people living in the United States, but also from residents of foreign countries as far away as India. I also received phone calls and e-mails not connected to my website, asking questions about grammar and suggesting things that I did not include in the book. All of this made it possible for me to understand where readers were coming from and some of the grammatical issues that were puzzling them.

This softbound edition is nearly identical with the original hardback, except for one primary change: in this new edition I have included an appendix titled "Keeping Up-To-Date: Ten Short Reminders." The appendix, based on the queries from my website, deals with recent changes in the accepted standards of grammar that many people are unaware of. It is my hope that these few pages at the end of the book will make this edition of *The Big Ten of Grammar* even more useful for people who care about the grammar they use.

Introduction

This book is *not* meant to be a complete guide for English grammar. It is only meant to help identify the ten grammatical errors that, in the opinion of this author, are the most frequently made and the most obvious. They are easy to recognize and to correct. And as you master the ten errors of English grammar discussed in this book, you will become a far better communicator, both personally and professionally. You will be amazed at the positive differences this will make in your life—at home, at work, and in the larger community.

Taking the time to be well informed about good grammar, and putting into practice what you have learned, will place you in a position where others will look up to you, will admire you as an effective communicator, and will pay more attention to what you are saying and writing. You will sense a new level of respect that others have for you.

A good friend of mine read an early draft of this book. Her initial reaction was that she had a very good grasp of grammar and did not need my book. But, as a favor to me, she read it anyway. She thought, "Chapter 1 is a no-brainer," which reinforced her initial reaction about her not needing the book. As she read the second chapter, however, she said, "Oh, my gosh, there are some errors I have been making." And as she continued to read other chapters, she concluded, "I *do* need this book."

Spending the few hours it will take you to understand and put into practice what this book is all about will definitely enhance your professional career, whether you are a high school student applying for college, a seasoned senior executive fulfilling your extensive responsibilities, or some place in the wide spectrum between the two. This is true especially during trying economic times, when the job market is unusually competitive. Your letters of application will be more convincing. Your departmental reports and executive summaries will be more distinctive. Your job interviews and personal conversations will have a different ring to them. Your understanding and use of good grammar will result in setting you apart from others. Whether writing or speaking, you will come across as a self-assured (not to be confused with cocky), articulate, and talented person who is able to get the job done.

People generally assume that grammar is so complicated that it would take far too much time and effort to study up on what they are doing wrong. However, identifying and correcting the ten most frequently made grammatical errors is not all that difficult. The misconception that it is, in my opinion, stems from several factors.

One is that when teaching English, we have historically emphasized learning rules and standards, and most people in today's hectic mode of life are just too busy meeting personal and professional commitments to take the time to memorize umpteen rules of grammar. But mastering basic grammar does not have to be difficult and time-consuming. I have found that in many instances it is not a matter of learning a bunch of grammatical rules. What is needed, instead, is *learning to listen to what you are saying.* Once you realize what you need to listen for, you will be amazed at how quickly you will detect and automatically correct typical grammatical errors.

Another problem is that most grammar books just do not meet the needs of the person looking for a brief refresher course that addresses basic practices of English grammar. English books today tend to go to one extreme or the other. Either they have so many pages and are so complicated that even the seasoned grammarian has trouble making sense of them, or they are so shallow in content or cutesy in presentation that they are of no use to the person who is serious about finding a reliable source for correcting the most frequently made grammatical errors. My goal in writing this book has been to avoid both of these pitfalls and to provide a practical, easy-to-use, and trustworthy resource that the average person will find understandable and helpful when brushing up on English grammar.

A third problem is that grammar books do not provide enough examples of correct and incorrect grammar. I discovered long ago as a teacher in the classroom that the person who is struggling to get a concept thoroughly in mind is helped by having a considerable number of examples, and the person who grasps the concept more quickly can skip the extra examples and move on to the next subject. I included many more examples of correct and incorrect sentences and various constructions of grammar than the typical book. There is no question that having numerous examples of both correct and incorrect usages of grammar and *reading them out loud* helps one develop his or her listening skills.

The most oft-repeated and prominent grammatical errors that people make can, in my opinion, be boiled down to ten. I never cease to be amazed at how frequently these same ten mistakes in grammar are made by people in all walks of life. They are conspicuous in advertisements, in movie and TV scripts, on websites, in news broadcasts and articles appearing in newspapers, and they are used by business and professional people, school teachers, parents and their children, politicians, seminar leaders, and on and on the list goes.

Each of these ten errors in grammar is addressed in this book. The bottom line is that brushing up on one's grammar and fixing these mistakes does not have to be difficult and time-consuming. That is why I wrote this book.

Before reading further, you have every right to ask, "What makes you an authority on the subject of grammar?" Two things.

When I graduated from high school and entered the University of Missouri as a freshman, one of the required courses was English 101. It soon became obvious to the instructor that I did not know the basic parts of speech and had a very limited understanding of English grammar. During the second week of the semester, the instructor—as I remember, her name was Mrs. Jones—asked me to stay after class to talk with her.

In those days, the instructors were very formal in addressing students, and I still remember her saying to me, "Mr. Bradshaw, you do not belong in this class." At first I did not understand the implication of her comment. I responded, "I think this is the right class, Mrs. Jones. This is English 101, isn't it?" She responded by saying, "Yes, this is English 101, and every freshman must take the class and make a passing grade in it."

She went on to explain to me that, in her judgment, I was not adequately prepared for the class and suggested that I withdraw. She was a kind woman and thought she was doing me a favor. She was trying to help me understand that, based on her experience as a university instructor, she was firmly convinced I would fail English 101, a required course. Hence, it would be better for me to withdraw from the university and go home at the beginning of the semester than be embarrassed by flunking out at the end of the semester.

Once I understood what she really meant, I explained that there was one really big problem with this. "Even if I did agree with you, Mrs. Jones, my father would never stand for it. And let me tell you, one just doesn't disagree with that man. What he says goes! You and I, Mrs. Jones, have to figure out some way for me to stay at the university." With that, she suggested that, if I were willing, she would tutor me twice a week. Needless to say, I was willing. I spent endless hours working with her and doing literally hundreds of exercises in grammar that she had me struggle with on my own.

She did not give many small quizzes in her class. Grades for the semester primarily depended on class participation and the grade on the final exam. You can well imagine the pressure I was feeling as the semester drew to a close.

The final exam consisted of fifty sentences. The instructions were simple: "Correct any errors you find in the sentences." I was the last person to hand in my exam. I stayed until the very end of the test period. I tried and tried to find more errors, but I ended up making only one minor change in one of the fifty sentences. I could find no revisions to make in the other forty-nine. I was certain I had failed the exam.

Actually, all fifty of the sentences as they appeared on the exam were correct, and I made, by far, the highest grade in the class. Her fifty sentences were long and complex, involving some of the most difficult sentence structures and uses of grammar that one could possibly imagine. I had learned the correct rules of grammar for almost every conceivable situation and proved that I knew how to apply them under pressure.

Second, I earned my PhD from the University of St. Andrews in Scotland. Writing an acceptable thesis for a Scottish university required my learning the British rules and standards for English grammar, which are somewhat different from those in the United States. I studied under Matthew Black, principal of St. Mary's College at the university. Dr. Black was notorious for his attention to grammatical correctness. I still remember a lengthy conversation we had on the difference between using "often" and "frequently." I assure you that writing a 389-page thesis under the scrutiny of Dr. Black qualifies me to speak authoritatively about English grammar.

All in all, I have a very thorough and practical grasp of both American English and British English.

I do not claim to be infallible. When I do not know something, I am quick to admit it and reach for the current edition of *The Chicago Manual of Style: The Essential Guide for Writers, Editors, and Publishers*, a 1,026-page book published by the University of Chicago Press and considered by most people to be the premier authority on grammar in print today, and for the current edition of *Merriam-Webster's Collegiate Dictionary*, in my opinion the best dictionary on the market for everyday use. Although *The Associated Press Stylebook* is certainly worth looking at and is popular among journalists, I do not find it a consistently reliable resource for accurate answers to difficult grammatical questions.

People also should be careful about relying on their old high school or college grammar books. Although generally accepted practices of grammar are slow to change, over a period of time rules and practices do shift in emphases and gradually change. Grammar books twenty-five years old or older should not be considered a trustworthy guide for all current grammatical practices. And believe me, you certainly cannot trust the "spelling and grammar" programs on computers to be the final authority for correct grammar. There are too many times such programs are just flat-out incorrect.

It will be helpful, though not absolutely necessary, to read the chapters in order, rather than skipping around. The chapters are arranged in a logical sequence, with the early chapters focusing on those errors in grammar that are often repeated and are of a more flagrant nature, and the later chapters looking at the less glaring types of grammatical errors (but they are errors that need to be corrected). Other writers may disagree with my selection and the order in which I have arranged the chapters. But I assure you that if you decide to master the ten errors of English grammar discussed in this book, the rewards you reap will be many.

In addition to the ten chapters that deal with mistakes that many people make rather regularly in their daily lives, I have added what I call a bonus section. It is divided into four sections and has to do with exceptions to the general rules of grammar and unusual and complex usages of grammar that most of us are not faced with on a daily basis. But when we are confronted by these "out of the norm" grammatical situations, as most of us are from time to time, the materials in the bonus section are available in an easy-to-find format. Even the experienced grammarian is not expected to have all of these references memorized, references that can take hours to research. Personally, I don't like having my train of thought interrupted by having to search for the answer to a grammatical dilemma. So I keep the materials in the bonus section close at hand for easy access.

Chapter 1

The Number One Mistake: Misusing "I" and "Me"

Part A: Deleting the Other Person's Name

It is my observation that the single greatest error in grammar is the use of "I" instead of "me." This probably stems from the practice of many grade-school teachers stressing the use of "I" instead of "me"—you know, don't say "Jim and me went to the ball game," but "Jim and I" did such and such. But there are many times that it is correct to use "me" instead of "I."

The problem arises primarily when using "I" or "me" with another person's name. Below are some examples of what I am referring to, all of which I have heard people use.

> "You are the best thing that ever happened to your dad and I." **This is incorrect.**

> **It should be:** "You are the best thing that ever happened to your dad and me."

As pointed out above, the problem comes when using "I" or "me" with another name—in this case "your dad." To show you what I mean, take out "your dad," and say the sentence again.

"You are the best thing that ever happened to I." You would never say that.

Instead, you would say, "You are the best thing that ever happened to me."

Follow suit when including "your dad" in the sentence: "You are the best thing that ever happened to your dad and me."

You do not need to learn rules about using various parts of speech to know whether to use "I" or "me" with "your dad." Your ear tells you that in this case it should be "me."

Let's look at another example.

"They were friendly with Susan and I." **Incorrect.**

"They were friendly with Susan and me." **Correct.**

The trouble comes when using "I" or "me" with "Susan." Take out Susan's name, and let your ear tell you whether you should use "I" or "me."

You would never say, "They were friendly with I."

Instead, you would naturally say, "They were friendly with me."

Once you have identified that it should be "me," put "Susan" back into the sentence. Hence, you should say, "They were friendly with Susan and me."

It's just that easy—not trying to remember rules of grammar, but listening to what you are saying.

Let's look at another example. Think in terms of what you would say if you were referring only to yourself and not to you and someone else.

"They expect to bring the other things to Fred and I." **Incorrect.**

"They expect to bring the other things to Fred and me." **Correct.**

Take "Fred" out of the sentence, and you would never say, "They expect to bring the other things to I."

So when you put "Fred" back into the sentence, just follow suit and say, "They expect to bring the other things to Fred and me."

Since using "I" instead of "me" is such a frequently made grammatical error, let's look at another example.

"Jim talked with Ken and I about the report."
Incorrect.

"Jim talked with Ken and me about the report."
Correct.

Take "Ken" out of the sentence, and you would never say, "Jim talked with I about the report."

So when you put "Ken" back into the sentence, you should say, "Jim talked with Ken and me about the report."

Let us look at one more example of using "I" or "me."

"You gave Isabelle and I just what we needed."
Incorrect.

It should be: "You gave Isabelle and me just what we needed."

Remember, the problem comes when using "I" or "me" with another name—in this case "Isabelle." Take out "Isabelle," and say the sentence again.

You would never say, "You gave I just what I needed."

Instead, you would say, "You gave me just what I needed."

Follow suit when using Isabelle: "You gave Isabelle and me just what we needed."

In most instances, you do not need to learn a bunch of rules about various parts of speech to know whether to use "I" or "me" in a sentence. Usually, your ear will tell you which to use.

At first, you may find it a little cumbersome, especially when you are speaking and not writing, to stop and think ahead of time about what your sentence should sound like. But if you practice just a little, you will be surprised at how quickly you will develop an ear for what you should be saying as soon as you begin to craft a sentence in your mind. Even when you are speaking and do not have the time to pause and think about which way it should be, a little practice developing your listening skills will reap humongous gains much more quickly than you could have imagined.

Below are five more sentences that I have heard other people say. Each is an example of using "I" or "me" with another person's name. I have indicated only that using "I" in each sentence is incorrect. I have left it to the reader to work though the process of eliminating the additional person's name and thinking only of what you should hear if the sentence referred to you alone. When you have deleted the other person's name, in each of these examples your ear will tell you that you should use "me" instead of "I." Then put the extra name back into the sentence, and say the sentence again using "me." To help you with this exercise, in each of the first two examples I have put in parentheses what you would delete from the sentence. You are completely on your own on the remaining three sentences. Since this exercise is meant to help you develop better listening skills, it would be helpful for you to work through these sentences by saying them out loud.

> "When you act that way, how can you expect (your mother and) I to trust you?" **Incorrect.**

> "This idea came to (Daniel and) I at the same time." **Incorrect.**

> "Dad let my sister and I drive the car to the movie." **Incorrect.**

"Our friends invited Linda and I to come to their house for dinner." **Incorrect.**

"I thought we agreed to give Amy time to adjust to you and I." **Incorrect.**

There are, of course, many times that it is correct to use "I" instead of "me." Again, your ear will tell you to use "I" instead of "me" in the following examples.

"Shirley and me reported to the group." **Incorrect.**

"Shirley and I reported to the group." **Correct.**

Take "Shirley" out of the sentence, and you would never say, "Me reported to the group."

Instead, you would say, "I reported to the group."

Put "Shirley" back into the sentence and follow suit: "Shirley and I reported to the group."

"The group asked to hear the report that Shirley and me prepared." **Incorrect.**

"The group asked to hear the report that Shirley and I prepared." **Correct.**

Take "Shirley" out of the sentence, and you would never say, "The group asked to hear the report that me prepared."

Instead, you would say, "The group asked to hear the report that I prepared."

Put "Shirley" back into the sentence and follow suit: "The group asked to hear the report that Shirley and I prepared."

"Dan and me listened carefully to the directions." **Incorrect.**

"Dan and I listened carefully to the directions."
Correct.

Take "Dan" out of the sentence. You would never say, "Me listened carefully to the directions."

Instead, you would say, "I listened carefully to the directions."

Put "Dan" back into the sentence and follow suit: "Dan and I listened carefully to the directions."

It is not a matter of learning rules of grammar. It is, instead, a matter of learning how to listen and letting your ear tell you whether you should use "I" or "me" in a sentence. In most instances, your ear will not lead you astray.

I suggest that you compose ten examples of your own and that all ten of the sentences use either "I" or "me" along with another person's name. With each example, be sure to think what it would sound like if you were only referring to yourself and not also to another person. As soon as you do that, you will know whether you should use "I" or "me." Your ear will tell you which one is correct.

Part B: Completing the Sentence

Thus far we have been emphasizing that many people use "I" or "me" incorrectly in a sentence when another person's name is also included. We have learned how easy it is to determine whether "I" or "me" should be used in a sentence by first eliminating the other person's name and then *hearing* whether to use "I" or "me." There is another equally easy (and sometimes necessary) way to determine in some sentences whether "I" or "me" is correct.

Sometimes one needs to complete the sentence in order to hear which is correct. Below is an example of what I mean.

"Jane writes better than me." **Incorrect.**

"Jane writes better than I." **Correct.**

In this instance, one needs to complete the sentence to hear which is correct.

"Jane writes better than me writes." You would never say that.

Instead, you would say, "Jane writes better than I write."

Once you complete the sentence, your ear quickly tells you that using "I" in this sentence is correct. It should be: "Jane writes better than I."

I want to repeat something here: sometimes you need to complete the sentence in order to hear whether "I" or "me" is correct. Remember that we are still focused on hearing what is correct. But there is a big problem here. Since "I" and "me" are used incorrectly so much of the time, what your ear tells you may be misleading. Your ear may be too accustomed to hearing the wrong thing. Therefore, sometimes it is necessary to complete the sentence before you can hear correctly whether to use "I" or "me."

Let's look at another example.

"My older brother runs faster than me." **Incorrect.**

"My older brother runs faster than I." **Correct.**

Again, if you *complete the sentence*, your ear will tell you that "I" is correct.

"My older brother runs faster then me runs." That sounds really silly.

Instead, you would say, "My older brother runs faster than I run."

It is not uncommon for people to rationalize that sometimes it is better to use "me" even though they know that "I" should be used. They reason that the correct form is so unfamiliar that most people would think they were being incorrect when, in fact, they were saying it correctly. Hence, they intentionally use the incorrect form.

In order to get around this problem in cases where the incorrect word is used frequently, just get in the habit of completing the sentence in the first place. Instead of saying, "My older brother runs faster than I," say, "My older brother runs faster than I run" or "My older brother runs faster than I do." If you craft your sentence in this way from the beginning, those who do not know the correct word to use, but mistakenly think they do, will not fault you, and those who do know the correct form will applaud the fact that you have a thorough grasp of grammatical rules and are able to apply them. That's a real win-win solution.

Here's another example.

> "Bill has a better tan than me." **Incorrect.**

> "Bill has a better tan than I." **Correct.**

If you complete the sentence, your ear will tell you whether to use "I" or "me."

> "Bill has a better tan than me has." Your ear tells you that "me" is **incorrect.**

> "Bill has a better tan than I have." Your ear tells you that "I" is **correct.**

I have included several more examples because so many people have trouble with the correct use of "I" or "me" in sentences similar to the following examples.

> "Shirley is prettier than me." **Incorrect.**

> "Shirley is prettier than I." **Correct.**

Complete the sentence.

"Shirley is prettier than me am pretty." When you complete the sentence, your ear tells you not to say "me am pretty."

"Shirley is prettier than I am pretty." When you complete the sentence, your ear tells you it is correct to use "I" instead of "me" in this sentence: "Shirley is prettier than I."

"He drives faster than me." **Incorrect.**

"He drives faster than I." **Correct.**

Complete the sentence.
"He drives faster than me drives." Your ear quickly tells you "me" is incorrect.
"He drives faster than I drive." Your ear tells you that "I" is correct. So the sentence should be: "He drives faster than I."

"My brother is like me." **Incorrect.**

"My brother is like I." **Correct.**

Again, complete the sentence.
"My brother is like me am." That is clearly incorrect.
"My brother is like I am." Your ear tells you this is correct.

"He rides like me." **Incorrect.**

"He rides like I." **Correct.**

Complete the sentence and you will readily hear why "I" is correct.
"He rides like me rides." That's a no-brainer. You would never say that.
"He rides like I ride." Clearly, using "I" in this case is correct.
This next example caught my attention during a major-network interview with a nationally known politician.

"It is a difficult thing for a person like me to see this happening." **Incorrect.**

"It is a difficult thing for a person like I to see this happening." **Correct.**

How do we know that using "me" is incorrect? Apply the principle we have been focusing on: complete the sentence, or in this case, complete that part of the sentence that relates to the use of "I" or "me."

"It is a difficult thing for a person like me am to see this happening." You would never say "me am." Your ear clearly tells you that "me am" is incorrect and that "I am" is correct.

I suspect the majority of casual listeners, prior to applying the test of completing the sentence, would think that using "me" in this sentence is correct. Sometimes your ear is so accustomed to hearing what is incorrect that it is necessary to complete the sentence in order to hear what is actually correct.

Here are two more examples of getting mixed up on whether to use "I" or "me." The first is from a national advertising campaign that was broadcast on network and independent TV stations, and the other is from an afternoon talk show of a major TV network. Again, I suspect that the great majority of people looking at these two sentences would initially think that the correct examples are incorrect and vice versa. These are good examples of our ears being so accustomed to hearing the wrong thing that we need to complete the sentences (or those parts of the sentences that pertain to the use of "I" or "me") in order *to hear* whether to use "I" or "me."

"If you are busy like me, then stay tuned." **Incorrect.**

"If you are busy like I, then stay tuned." **Correct.**

Complete the first part of the sentence to hear whether to use "I" or "me."

"If you are busy like me am busy, then stay tuned." Clearly incorrect.

"If you are busy like I am busy, then stay tuned." No doubt about it. Your ear tells you that using "I" is correct.

"There are many people who think like me about this." **Incorrect.**

"There are many people who think like I about this." **Correct.**

Complete the last part of the sentence to hear whether to use "I" or "me."

"There are many people who think like me thinks about this." Your ear clearly tells you that using "me" in this sentence is incorrect.

"There are many people who think like I think about this." Correct.

Below are five more examples. I have indicated only that in each of these sentences using "me" is incorrect. I have left it to you to work through completing the sentences and then letting your ear tell you that using "I" is correct in each of them. Again, since you are developing your listening skills, I encourage you to work through these sentences out loud.

"I want to hear from those of you who think like me." **Incorrect.**

"He makes better speeches than me." **Incorrect.**

"Richard did better than me on the exam." **Incorrect.**

"Karen works harder than me." **Incorrect.**

"My brother looks like me." **Incorrect.**

You need merely to complete the sentences to hear whether to use "I" or "me."

To recap, in this chapter we have learned the following:

✓ Many people use "I" when they should use "me."

✓ This happens most frequently when another person's name is also being used in the sentence.

✓ It is easy to determine whether "I" or "me" should be used in a sentence by first eliminating the other person's name and then *hearing* whether to use "I" or "me."

✓ Sometimes it is necessary to complete the sentence in order *to hear* whether to use "I" or "me."

✓ It is important to learn how to hear what you are saying even as you are crafting a sentence.

Special note about "like" and "than"

Scholars have been debating the proper uses of "like" and "than" since about 1560. The disagreements primarily center on two issues: (1) whether "like" and "than" should be used as prepositions or conjunctions and (2) whether the nouns and pronouns following "like" and "than" should be used in the objective or the nominative case. Most of us find these issues to be confusing, time-consuming, and intimidating. Hopefully this book will eliminate the need for guessing.

Most scholars today agree that using "than" as I suggest in this chapter is *the* correct usage and that my way of using "like" is also grammatically correct, although not necessarily the *only* correct way. My method provides a consistent way of avoiding all the uncertainty by (1) completing the sentence, (2) applying the listening test, and (3) letting our ears tell us the correct usage of "like" and "than" and their accompanying nouns and pronouns. Doing these three things every time we question the proper way to use "like" or "than" eliminates the need for time-consuming deliberation and always provides us with grammatically correct sentences.

Chapter 2

Working with "He" or "Him" and "She" or "Her"

Although the kinds of grammatical mistakes we have been talking about in the first chapter happen most frequently when using "I" or "me," the same types of errors also occur when using "he" or "him" and "she" or "her" with other words. And, again, your ear will tell you which word to use.

Let's look at some examples.

"I talked with he and his wife." **Incorrect.**

"I talked with him and his wife." **Correct.**

What we discussed in chapter 1 applies here. You don't need rules of grammar to know whether to use "he" or "him" in the sentence. The problem comes primarily when using "he" or "him" with another person—in this case "his wife." Delete "and his wife," and say the sentence again. Your ear will tell you whether to use "he" or "him."

You would never say, "I talked with he."

Instead, your ear will tell you to say, "I talked with him."

Follow suit when including "and his wife": "I talked with him and his wife."

When you remove "his wife" from the sentence, your ear automatically tells you to use "him" in this sentence. Here's another one.

"Everyone liked the report that him and Kimberly presented." **Incorrect.**

"Everyone liked the report that he and Kimberly presented." **Correct.**

If you take "Kimberly" out of the sentence, your ear tells you that "he" is correct.

You would never say, "Everyone liked the report that him presented."

Instead, you would say, "Everyone liked the report that he presented."

Put "and Kimberly" back into the sentence, and follow suit: "Everyone liked the report that he and Kimberly presented."

Let's try this one.

"Alice's grandmother reminds me of she and your mother." **Incorrect.**

"Alice's grandmother reminds me of her and your mother." **Correct.**

You would never say, "Alice's grandmother reminds me of she."

Instead, you would say, "Alice's grandmother reminds me of her."

Follow suit when including "and your mother" in the sentence: "Alice's grandmother reminds me of her and your mother."

Here are two examples that demonstrate a frequently made grammatical error.

"Her and her husband are coming by to see us." **Incorrect.**

"She and her husband are coming by to see us." **Correct.**

Take out "and her husband" and you will readily hear that "she" is correct.

"Her is coming by to see us." That sounds ridiculous.

"She is coming by to see us." No question—"she" is correct.

> "Her and her little friend got home at the time promised." **Incorrect.**

> "She and her little friend got home at the time promised." **Correct.**

Take out "her little friend" and you will hear that "she" is correct.

"Her got home at the time promised." This is clearly wrong.

"She got home at the time promised." Your ear tells you "she" is correct.

Thus far in this chapter, we have concentrated on determining whether to use "he" or "him" or "she" or "her" with another person's name by temporarily deleting the name of the other person and letting your ear tell you which pronoun to use and then putting the other person's name back into the sentence. But, applying another principle we learned in chapter 1, sometimes a person needs to complete the sentence in order *to hear* whether "her" or "she" or "him" or "he" is correct. Let's look at some examples. And remember, you are honing your listening skills, so say these sentences out loud.

> "No one runs as fast as him." **Incorrect.**

> "No one runs as fast as he." **Correct.**

Complete the sentence, and listen for what is correct.

"No one runs as fast as him runs." That sounds really stupid. Instead, you would say, "No one runs as fast as he runs." Hence, you would say, "No one runs as fast as he." Or, try this one.

"These people are like her." **Incorrect.**

"These people are like she." **Correct.**

Complete the sentence, and you'll hear that using "she" is correct.

"These people are like her is." Your ear tells you "her" is wrong.

"These people are like she is." No question about it—"she" is correct.

Hence, the correct form of the sentence is "These people are like she."

Let's try another one. I heard it used by a newscaster on a major TV network.

"Her son is taller than her." **Incorrect.**

"Her son is taller than she." **Correct.**

Complete the sentence in order to hear whether "her" or "she" is correct.

"Her son is taller than her is tall." Even the newscaster wouldn't have said that. When you complete the sentence, your ear will tell you what to say.

"Her son is taller than she is tall." You can hear that using "she" is correct. Hence, you should say, "Her son is taller than she."

Many people seem to get this next one wrong. But if you take the time to complete the sentence, there will be no question in your mind as to the correct word to use.

"I want to be just like her." **Incorrect.**

"I want to be just like she." **Correct.**

Complete the sentence.

"I want to be just like her is." That doesn't sound right. Let's try it again.

"I want to be just like she is." That's it! Your ear clearly tells you "she" is correct. Hence, you should say, "I want to be just like she."

Here are four more examples that are problematic for many people. The last two are identical except one uses the masculine pronoun and the other uses the feminine. I have heard these sentences, or ones very similar to them, used frequently—and many times the wrong pronoun is used. When we complete the sentences, the right pronouns are easy to hear.

"Everyone wants to be better than her." **Incorrect.**

"Everyone wants to be better than she." **Correct.**

Complete the sentence.

"Everyone wants to be better than her is." You hear that "her" is incorrect.

"Everyone wants to be better than she is." No question— "she" is correct.

"I sure wish I could hit the ball like him."
Incorrect.

"I sure wish I could hit the ball like he." **Correct.**

Again, complete the sentence.

"I sure wish I could hit the ball like him hits it." Clearly, "him" is wrong.

"I sure wish I could hit the ball like he hits it." No question—"he" is correct.

"I ride like him." **Incorrect.**

"I ride like he." **Correct.**

Complete the sentence and you will readily hear that "he" is correct.

"I ride like him rides." That's enough to break your eardrum.

"I ride like he rides." Clearly, "he" is correct.

"I ride like her." **Incorrect.**

"I ride like she." **Correct.**

Complete the sentence and you will hear that "she" is correct.

"I ride like her rides." Using "her" sounds silly.

"I ride like she rides." Using "she" is correct.

The next is an example of a sentence in which the part needing to be completed is in the middle of the sentence rather than at the end. Completing that part of the sentence may be more difficult than completing the end of a sentence, but it works the same way.

"How did a guy like him get promoted?" **Incorrect.**

"How did a guy like he get promoted?" **Correct.**

Complete the part of the sentence that is applicable.

"How did a guy like him is get promoted?" You would not say "like him is."

"How did a guy like he is get promoted?" Clearly, using "he" is correct.

Although this chapter focuses on the proper use of "he" or "him" and "she" or "her," completing the sentence is also a very effective technique for deciding the proper use of other pronouns. See the following example about whether to use "we" or "us."

"He said to his wife, 'Most of the people here are younger than us.'" **Incorrect.**

"He said to his wife, 'Most of the people here are younger than we.'" **Correct.**

At first, your ear may tell you that "us" is correct, but if you complete the sentence, you will hear that "we" is correct. Listen to how out of place "us" sounds.

"He said to his wife, 'Most of the people here are younger than us are.'"

"He said to his wife, 'Most of the people here are younger than we are.'"

When you complete the sentence, there is absolutely no question that "we" should be used in this sentence.

Many of the above examples are similar to what we discussed in chapter 1, where it was pointed out that sometimes just listening for what is right is not enough. When a wrong usage of a word has become very prevalent, just applying the listening test may be misleading. You may be so accustomed to hearing the wrong thing that your ear mistakenly tells you that the wrong thing is correct.

In such instances it is extremely helpful—even *necessary* until you retrain your ear to recognize correct usage—to complete the sentence before applying the listening test. If you complete the sentence before applying the listening test, when you do apply the listening test, your ear will tell you what is and is not correct.

It makes sense in such cases, in order to derail any misunderstanding from the outset, to develop the habit of completing the sentence not only in your mind, but also when you are actually saying or writing it. Instead of saying "I ride like he," say "I ride like he rides" or "I ride like he does." If you complete the sentence in the first place, even those who would mistakenly assume that it is correct to say or write "I ride like him" will hear that "I ride like he rides" is actually correct and will give the matter no further thought. If you fail to complete the sentence when you are saying it in the first place, the untrained ear may *mistakenly* tell you that using "him" is correct.

To recap, in this chapter we stressed the following:

✓ We do not need to learn rules of grammar in order to determine for most sentences the correct usages of "he" or "him" and "she" or "her." Instead, we need to learn to listen for what is correct.

✓ When using a pronoun with another person's name, sometimes we can *hear* what pronoun to use by temporarily deleting the other person's name from the sentence.

✓ Other times it will be necessary to complete the sentence *to hear* what is correct.

✓ One of the best ways to learn to listen is by reading the many examples *out loud*.

See the special note on page 20 for a reminder of the correct uses of "like" and "than." The three things I recommend on page 20 to make certain that you always use "like" and "than" correctly with "I" and "me" also should be applied when deciding whether to use "like" or "than" with "he" and "him" and with "she" and "her." The three things I recommend are (1) complete the sentence, (2) apply the listening test, and (3) let your ears tell you the correct usage of "like" or "than" and their accompanying nouns and pronouns.

Chapter 3

Quotation Marks and Other Punctuation

In this chapter we depart from concentrating on developing listening skills and turn to developing writing skills. In the previous two chapters it was stressed that rules of grammar did not have to be learned—that someone would know automatically what rules of grammar should be followed by listening. This chapter, however, addresses the correct placement of quotation marks when they are used in sentences with periods, commas, colons, semicolons, question marks, and exclamation marks. Whether a comma comes before or after quotation marks is not something one can determine by listening; the sentence will sound the same regardless of the placement of the comma (or other punctuation) in relation to the quotation marks. It is necessary, therefore, to learn and remember three rules. They are simple rules, but many people violate them.

I ask the reader to memorize grammatical rules and standards only when it is absolutely necessary. Chapter 3 is one of those cases in which learning rules is necessary. In such instances, I include examples not only to help you understand the subject matter being discussed, but also as a means of remembering or recalling at a later time what needs to be remembered. I suggest, therefore, that you pay very careful attention to these examples and practice recalling them so it will be easier for you to remember the three rules being referred to.

In the United States there are *absolutely no exceptions* to the following three rules of grammar dealing with quotation marks.

✓ Commas or periods *always* precede closing quotation marks of quoted material. See the following examples.

> In this city you will find some "Republicans," some "Democrats," and some "Independents."
>
> He said "no," and she said "yes."
>
> There are no "ifs," "ands," or "buts" about it.
>
> When you say, "I love you," it makes me know I really "lucked out."

✓ Colons and semicolons *always* follow closing quotation marks of quoted material. See the following examples.

> Some people call themselves "Republicans"; some call themselves "Democrats"; and some call themselves "Independents."
>
> He said "no"; she said "yes"; and some said neither "yes" nor "no."
>
> Every line of every verse ends with the same word in Charles Wesley's Easter hymn "Christ the Lord is Risen Today": "Alleluia!"
>
> Take, for example, the song "America"; it is also called "My Country, 'Tis of Thee."

✓ Question marks and exclamation points always follow closing quotation marks unless the question mark or exclamation point belongs to the material being quoted, in which case the question mark or exclamation point precedes the closing quotation marks.

Sometimes it can be confusing whether the question mark or exclamation point goes before or after the closing quotation marks. Let us look at some examples.

Did she say, "How many people are here"?

Since the entire sentence is a question, the question mark belongs at the very end of the sentence, after the quotation marks.

She said, "How many people are here?"

Unlike the previous example, the entire sentence is not a question; *only the quoted material is a question*. Hence, the question mark belongs only to the quote and must remain within the quotation marks.

Who asked, "Did you make that decision"?

Again, *since the entire sentence is a question,* the question mark belongs at the very end of the sentence, after the closing quotation marks.

Bill said, "Did you make that decision?"

In this case *the entire sentence is not a question.* The question relates only to that part of the sentence that is within the quotation marks. Hence, the question mark belongs to the quoted material, must remain within the quotation, and, therefore, precedes the closing quotation marks.

That house is a "Wow"!

Since the entire sentence is exclamatory, the exclamation point is at the very end of the sentence, after the quotation marks.

> When she saw the new house, she said, "Wow!"

Unlike the previous sentence, the exclamation is not part of the entire sentence, but *relates only to the quote*. Hence, the exclamation point belongs to the quote and, therefore, precedes the closing quotation marks.

> She screamed, "Stop the car!"

The exclamation point belongs to the quote, not to the entire sentence.

These three rules apply to the use of both double and single quotation marks. Double quotation marks are the standard to use for regular quotes, and single quotation marks are the standard for designating a quote within a quote. One should punctuate single quotation marks the same as double ones, except that the double marks should always be placed outside of the single marks at both the beginning and close of a quote. The following examples correctly use single quotation marks for quotes within a quote and illustrate the correct placement of double quotation marks outside single ones.

> As she was telling others of her experience, Nancy said, "When the fireman asked me, 'Are you all right?' I replied, 'Yes, I think so.'"

Within the sentence, there is a long quote by Nancy that is set off by double quotation marks. Within this primary quote, there are two shorter quotes, one in the middle of the sentence and the other at the end of the sentence, each of which is set off by single quotation marks. In the first part of the sentence when the fireman asked a question, *the single quotation mark follows the question mark*, just as it would if they were double quotation marks. At the end of the sentence, *the single quotation mark follows the period,* as would be the case with double quotation marks, and the *double quotation marks follow the single mark.*

> Her husband said, "When I saw that she was safely out of the building, I fell to my knees and quoted from Thomas Ken's famous doxology hymn sung to the tune 'Old Hundredth': 'Praise God, from whom all blessings flow.'"

Again, there are within the sentence a primary quotation set off by double quotation marks and two sets of single quotation marks within the primary quotation. The first set of single quotation marks is used to specify a specific tune. As would be the case with double quotation marks, *the colon* (:) *follows the single quotation mark* ('Old Hundredth':). At the end of the second set of single quotation marks, which is at the end of the sentence, the *single quotation mark follows the period,* just as would be the case with double quotation marks, and the *double quotation marks follow the single one.*

The next example is comprised of a short paragraph rather than a single sentence.

> Realizing how difficult it can be to resist temptation, a young man told his priest, "I can identify with St. Paul when he said, 'The spirit is willing, but the flesh is weak.'" The young man continued. "I have a question for you, Father: 'Is it possible to overcome temptation?' That is what I want to know."

In this paragraph, there are two regular quotations set off by double quotation marks, and within each of the two regular quotations there is a quotation set off by single marks. The single quotation marks adhere to the same rules and standards of grammar as would be used if they were double marks, and the double quotation marks are placed outside the single ones.

Please remember that at the beginning of this chapter it was emphasized that in the United States there are absolutely no exceptions to these three rules of grammar dealing with quotation marks. In Great Britain and countries settled by England, however, the rules and standards for using punctuation marks with quotation marks differ from those in the United States in two ways: (1) all punctuation marks—the comma, period, colon, semicolon, question mark, and exclamation point—always follow the closing quotation marks; and (2) usually single quotation marks are used for all regular quotations, and double quotation marks are used for quotes within a quote. These make no difference to the average person living in the United States. But if you are doing business with a company located in a foreign country, as more and more Americans are, you may wonder when sending a letter to a foreign business whether to follow the rules of grammar used in the United States or those used by the foreign country to which the communiqué is being sent.

My advice is that one should always use the grammar of his or her own country. Businesses in other countries do not expect you to change your writing habits for them any more than the average American is offended or put off by receiving a letter from a person or company located in another country in which the accepted standards of grammar of that country are used. Unless you are writing some formal proclamation for a head of state, for a formal state occasion, or some other very important circumstance, it is better, in my opinion, to stick to the grammar that you are accustomed to using. Otherwise, you are likely to make embarrassing errors. Of course, in foreign countries that have been greatly influenced by the United States, for example Japan and the Philippines, it is not a problem, as American English is primarily used in such countries instead of European English.

To recap, chapter 3 deals with the use of punctuation with quotation marks. There are three rules relating to quotation marks that need to be remembered. If you master these three simple rules of grammar, you will be among the few people who consistently punctuate quotations correctly in your written communiqués. The three rules are as follows:

- ✓ Commas or periods *always* precede closing quotation marks of quoted material. Of the three rules, this one is violated more frequently than the other two.

- ✓ Colons and semicolons *always* follow closing quotation marks of quoted material.

- ✓ Question marks and exclamation points always follow closing quotation marks *unless* the question mark or exclamation point belongs to the material being quoted, in which case the question mark or exclamation point precedes the closing quotation marks.

Chapter 4

The "ing" Thing

In this chapter we are dealing with what I call the "ing" thing. Learning to cope correctly with the "ing" thing requires learning another rule. Once you learn the rule, however, you will develop an ear for what should be said, and in most cases you will be able to forget the rule and depend on your ear to tell you which is the correct grammar to use.

What do I mean by the "ing" thing? I am referring to words that express action (referred to in grammar books as verbs) that have "ing" added to end of them. There are thousands of verbs in the English language, and the following few examples are meant to demonstrate how the "ing" thing is formed.

Action word (verb)	Adding "ing"
be	being
fly	flying
offer	offering
shout	shouting
take	taking
taste	tasting
try	trying
work	working

Here's the rule: when an action word ending in "ing" is immediately preceded by a person's name or by a personal pronoun, the person's name or pronoun is *usually* (not always) in the possessive case. That sounds complicated, but it's really not. Here are two examples of what I mean, the first using someone's name and the second using a personal pronoun.

> "I appreciate Nancy working so hard when I was on vacation." **Incorrect.**

"Nancy" immediately precedes "working," an action word ending in "ing." "Nancy" should be in the possessive case. The possessive case—denoting ownership or possession—of a person's name is formed by adding an apostrophe *s*. This sentence should be "I appreciate *Nancy's* working so hard when I was on vacation."

> "I am grateful for you taking time to see me."
> **Incorrect.**

Many people make the mistake of using "you" in this sentence, but using "you" (the regular form of a personal pronoun) in this sentence is incorrect. Rules of English call for a personal pronoun before an action word ending in "ing" to be in the possessive case in the majority of sentences. In this sentence "you" should be "your." The sentence should be "I am grateful for *your* taking time to see me."

For those of you who may have forgotten what a personal pronoun is, a personal pronoun is a word used as a substitute for a person's name. The possessive case of a personal pronoun denotes ownership or possession. There are very few personal pronouns in the English language. Below are listed *all* the personal pronouns in the English language and their possessive forms.

Personal pronoun	Possessive pronoun
I or me	my
you	your
he or him	his
she or her	her
we or us	our
they	their

Below are examples of incorrect and correct usages of personal pronouns with the "ing" thing.

"She expressed gratitude for me taking time to see her." **Incorrect.**

"She expressed gratitude for *my* taking time to see her." **Correct.** Use the possessive case of the personal pronoun before the "ing" thing.

"I appreciate him being so careful." **Incorrect.**

"I appreciate *his* being so careful." **Correct.** Use the possessive case of the personal pronoun before the "ing" thing.

"I think it's worth you making the effort to resolve the problem." **Incorrect.**

"I think it's worth *your* making the effort to resolve the problem." **Correct.** Possessive case of personal pronoun before the "ing" thing.

"She won't like me being gone for so long." **Incorrect.**

"She won't like *my* being gone for so long." **Correct.** Possessive case.

"I can see us offering a broad range of products." **Incorrect.**

"I can see *our* offering a broad range of products."
Correct. Possessive case.

"I appreciate him trying to help me." **Incorrect.**

"I appreciate *his* trying to help me." **Correct.** Possessive case.

"Your mother and I appreciate you coming home for Thanksgiving." **Incorrect.**

"Your mother and I appreciate *your* coming home for Thanksgiving." **Correct.** Possessive case.

"This wouldn't have happened without him giving his approval." **Incorrect.**

"This wouldn't have happened without *his* giving his approval." **Correct.** Possessive case.

In each of these examples, the attention is focused on the act, not the actor. That is the key thing to remember when dealing with the "ing" thing. When the attention or focus of the sentence is not on the actor but on what the actor does, the action word ending in "ing" qualifies as an "ing" thing. In such instances, a person's name or a personal pronoun immediately preceding the action word should be in the possessive case. Let's look at the correct form of each of these last eight examples again.

"She expressed gratitude for my taking time to see her." What is the gratitude for? Not for me, but for "taking time to see her." The gratitude does not focus on the person, but on what the person is doing—not on the actor, but on the act.

"I appreciate his being so careful." What is appreciated? Not the person, but what the person does: "being so careful." The focus is on the act, not the actor.

"I think it's worth your making the effort to resolve the problem." The attention is on "the effort to resolve the problem"—not on you but on what you are doing. The act, not the actor, is what is important.

"She won't like my being gone for so long." It is not that she won't like me; it is that she won't like what I am doing. The emphasis is on "being gone for so long," that is, on the act, not the actor.

"I can see our offering a broad range of products." What can I see? The emphasis is not on seeing us, but on "offering a broad range of products." The focus is on the act, not the actors.

"I appreciate his trying to help me." What is the focus here? "Trying to help me." The focus of the sentence is on the act, not the actor.

"Your mother and I appreciate your coming home for Thanksgiving." What is appreciated? Not you, but "your coming home for Thanksgiving." The focus is on the act, not the actor.

"This would not have happened without his giving his approval." What enabled "this" to happen? Not "him," but what he did: "giving his approval." The focus is on the act, not the actor. The "ing" thing is in play, and the possessive case is called for.

Not long ago I heard a rather well-known reporter on a major news network say the following:

> "I don't know which is more alarming: him not knowing that it was a problem or him not doing anything about it."

Both parts of the sentence after the colon are incorrect. It was not the man that was alarming, but what he was doing—the action, not the actor. What was alarming was "*his* not knowing it was a problem" and "*his* not doing anything about it." Clearly the "ing" thing is at play here.

Recently I heard the host of a popular radio talk show say this:

> "We appreciate you giving us a call."

This is clearly incorrect. The host of the radio show does not appreciate the caller, but appreciates what the caller did—she called in. The host was referring to the act, not the actor. The "ing" thing is in play. The sentence should be: "We appreciate *your* giving us a call."

The circulation department of a local newspaper thanked me for a trial subscription by telephoning me.

"We appreciate you giving our newspaper a try."

This is incorrect. The appreciation is not for me, but for what I did—that is, for "giving our newspaper a try." Again, the "ing" thing is in play, calling for the possessive case. The sentence should be "We appreciate *your* giving our newspaper a try."

When on the road recently, I spent a night at a motel operated by a well-known and popular international hotel company. I left a wake-up call for the next morning. When the telephone rang, the recorded message said,

"It is 6:00 a.m. We appreciate you staying with us and hope you will return."

The first use of "you" in this sentence is incorrect. What is appreciated? The appreciation is not for "you," but for what you did, that is, for "staying with us"—the act, not the actor. The possessive case is called for. "You" should be "your." "We appreciate *your* staying with us…"

Knowing the motel chain as I do, I suspect that the wording of the recorded message was handed down from corporate headquarters. If this is so, motels and hotels all over the United States and in several other countries are making the same mistake every morning.

It is disappointing that people who are in the public eye (or ear) are so sloppy or ignorant about correct grammar. If your career takes you to a position of public scrutiny, or if you are aspiring to such a career, you should prepare adequately for it.

And knowing and using proper grammar is part of that preparation. It is about having enough pride in what you're doing to do something about it!

Whenever the attention or focus of action is on the act instead of the actor, the "ing" thing comes into play, and the person's name or personal pronoun immediately preceding such an action word ending in "ing" should be in the possessive case. Those of you who are well-grounded in grammar will realize that what I am referring to as the "ing" thing is called a "gerund" in grammar books—that is, a verb ending in "ing" that is used as a noun, either as the subject or the object of the verb. When that is the case, the possessive form is used for the noun or pronoun immediately preceding the "ing" thing (gerund).

Sometimes, however, *the focus will be on the actor* and not the act. When that happens, the action word ending in "ing" is being used as a verb and not as a noun and does not qualify as the "ing" thing. Therefore, in such instances the regular form of the noun or pronoun—not the possessive case—is used before the action wording ending in "ing." Let's look at some examples.

> "The police officer called to the man crossing the street on a red light." **Correct.**

The emphasis is on "the man," not on "crossing the street"—on the actor, not on the act. The police officer did not speak or call out to the act; that is, he or she did not call to "crossing the street." The police officer called to the actor; that is, the police officer called to "the man." Since the attention is focused on the actor and not on the act, the "ing" thing does not apply here, and the regular form of "man," not the possessive form, is used.

"A man walking two dogs faces many problems."
Correct.

Again, the "ing" thing does not come into play because the focus of attention is on the actor, not on the act. Who is facing many problems in this sentence? The man—the actor—"faces many problems." The act—walking two dogs—is not facing problems. The dogs are not facing the problem. The attention of this sentence is on the actor—the man. Hence, this sentence is correct; the possessive case should not be used.

"Is Bill walking downtown?" **Correct.**

The "ing" thing is not present. The question focuses on Bill (the actor), not on "walking downtown" (the act). Is Bill walking? In this case, the importance of listening also comes back into play. Your ear tells you that you would *not* say, "Is Bill's walking downtown?" The possessive case is not used in this sentence.

"I am watching Alice baking a cake." **Correct.**

What am I watching? The sentence clearly states that I am watching Alice; the sentence does not say, "I am watching baking the cake." The attention is focused on Alice, not on "baking a cake"—that is, on the actor, not on the act. Hence, the possessive case of Alice is not used.

"We watched Nancy walking down the street."
Correct.

The "ing" thing does not come into play. In this sentence we are not watching "walking down the street." We are watching Nancy, who happens at the time to be walking down the street. The possessive case is not used.

To recap, these are the important things to take from this chapter:

✓ If an action word (a verb) ending in "ing" is immediately preceded by a person's name or a personal pronoun and focuses on or modifies the act and not the actor, the name or personal pronoun should be in the possessive case.

✓ If, on the other hand, the action word ending in "ing" refers to or modifies the actor and not the act, the name or personal pronoun immediately preceding the action word is *not* in the possessive case.

✓ Put another way, if the action word ending in "ing" is used as a noun—as the subject or object of the verb—the "ing" thing comes into play. If the action word ending in "ing" is used as a verb in the sentence, the "ing" thing does not come into play.

✓ The bottom line is this: *if the act is emphasized, possessive case is used; if the actor is emphasized, the possessive case is not used.*

Here are two final examples to show the difference.

"Your using a cane makes me feel better about leaving you alone."

Correct—possessive case. Why? Because what makes me feel better is not you, but what you are doing—"using a cane"—that is, the act and not the actor.

"Are you using your cane every day?"

Correct—not in possessive case. Why? Because the attention is focused on "you." The question is, "Are you doing something?" The question does not refer to what the cane is doing. In this sentence, "you" is the noun and "using" is the verb. The emphasis is on the actor, not the act. Your ear clearly tells you not to use the possessive—not to say, "Are your using your cane every day?"

I know that this may appear complicated. I think it is accurate to say that this chapter—dealing with the "ing" thing—is the most difficult of the entire book. But once you have practiced these sentences, your ear will begin to tell you what to listen for. You'll be amazed at how quickly you will not have to stop and think about whether or not to use the possessive form; it will come to you automatically as you are crafting the sentence. The importance of honing your listening skills surfaces again.

A final word: If you are not certain and just cannot make up your mind whether or not to use the possessive case of a name or personal pronoun before an action word ending in "ing" and you have to guess, you are more likely to be correct if you use the possessive form with a personal pronoun and the regular form with a person's name. Doing that will not guarantee that you always will be correct, but you are much more likely to be correct. If it gets down to having to guess, you probably would be wise to reword the sentence in such a way that there is no action word ending in "ing." For example, instead of having to decide between saying, "Your using a cane makes me feel better about leaving you alone" or "You using a cane makes me feel better about leaving you alone," say something like this: "When you use your cane, I feel better about leaving you alone."

Chapter 5

"That" or "Which" and Some Other Things

Today, with both the written and spoken word, "which" is frequently used when the correct usage calls for using "that." There is no good reason for making this mistake. It is very easy to distinguish when "that" should be used and when "which" should be used.

If it is information that is *essential* to the meaning of what is being said, you should use "that." If it is information that merely adds some *supplementary* information to something that has already been said, you should use "which." Put another way, "that" is used to narrow or identify a particular item being referred to. "Which" is used to add something about an item already identified.

Here are some examples of correct usage and why.

> "Dan's red car, which is parked in the garage, has a flat tire."

Dan's *red* car is what is being talked about. The implication in this sentence is that Dan has more than one car, and it is his *red* car that has a flat tire. The additional information about where Dan's red car is parked is not necessary to know which of Dan's cars is being referred to. Where the car is parked may be interesting information, but it is nonessential information. The thrust of this sentence is "Dan's red car has a flat tire." "Which" is correctly used in this sentence.

> "Dan's car that is parked in the garage has a flat tire."

The situation in this sentence is different. Where the car is parked is essential information for knowing which of Dan's cars has a flat tire. In this sentence, Dan has more than one car, only one of his cars is parked in the garage, and the one parked in the garage is the specific car that has the flat tire. "That" is correctly used in this sentence.

> "The front side of the house, which faces south, needs to be painted."

In this sentence, it is not necessary to know what direction the house faces. It is clear which side of the house needs to be painted: the front side. The fact that the front side of the house faces south is supplementary information; perhaps it is interesting information, but it is not needed to know which side of the house needs to be painted. "Which" is correct.

> "The side of the house that faces south needs to be painted."

The situation is different here. In this sentence, the specific side of the house needing to be painted is the south side. This is essential information. If we did not have this information, we would not know which side of the house needs to be painted. "That" is correct.

> "My new computer, which I take with me when traveling, is really easy to use."

There is no question what computer is being referred to—it is my new computer. The fact that I take it with me when traveling is supplementary information that may be interesting, but it is not information essential for knowing what computer is being referred to. "Which" is correct.

> "My computer that I take with me when traveling is really easy to use."

The implication in this sentence is that I have more than one computer, and I am referring specifically to the one that I take with me when traveling. Without the reference to traveling, one would not know which of my computers is being referred to. It is essential information. "That" is correct.

> "The master bedroom, which is on the first floor, has several windows."

It is clear that the master bedroom is the subject of the sentence. Where it is located is nonessential, supplementary information not needed to know what room in the house is being referred to. "Which" is correct.

> "The bedroom that is on the first floor has several windows."

This sentence suggests that there are two or more bedrooms in the house, but only one is located on the first floor. This sentence clearly refers to that one. It is necessary information in order to identify the specific bedroom being referred to. "That" is correct.

There is something else about these examples that needs to be noted. If you go back and examine the last eight examples, you will note that *all of the "which" phrases (expressions or groups of words) are set off by commas, and all of the "that" phrases are* not *set off by commas.* Make certain always to follow suit. Nonessential information is set off by commas, and essential information is not set off by commas.

This takes us beyond the use of "that" and "which." Whenever you use phrases that are not needed—that could be enclosed in parentheses or set apart by dashes—they should be set off by commas.

Let's look at some correct examples.

"My husband, Jack, is tall and has curly hair."

"Jack" is not needed. The sentence has already identified the person as "my husband." Adding "Jack" to the sentence merely tells us that, by the way, my husband's name is Jack. This is nonessential, supplementary information that is not needed to know who is being referred to. "Jack" is not needed and is, therefore, set off by commas.

"The house we live in, located on Second Street, is for sale."

The subject of the sentence is clearly "the house we live in." Where the house is located is supplementary information. It may be interesting to know where the house is located, but that information is not needed to identify what house is being referred to. Therefore, "located on Second Street" is nonessential information and is set off by commas.

"My daughter, Jane, is in high school."

It is clear in this sentence that my daughter is being referred to. The implication here is that there is only one daughter, and, by the way, her name is Jane. It may be nice to know that my daughter's name is Jane, but this is nonessential information. Therefore, "Jane" is set off by commas.

"My daughter Jane is in high school."

This is the same sentence as the previous one, except that this one has no commas. Having the sentence without commas can also be correct, but eliminating the commas makes the sentence take on a different meaning. What is the difference?

In the first sentence "Jane" is set off by commas. This sentence structure tells us that her name is nonessential information—interesting, but not necessary. This enables us to arrive at the conclusion that the only reason for her name being nonessential information is that there is only one daughter. Hence, knowing her name is not necessary.

By eliminating the commas, we may infer that Jane's name is essential to the meaning of the sentence. This sentence structure enables us to reason that there are two or more daughters and, therefore, that it is necessary to include the name of which daughter is being referred to. In this sentence, Jane's name is essential information and should not be set off by commas.

Many people do not pay much attention to commas. They just stick them in wherever it looks or sounds like it would be good to have a comma. But sentence structure—just putting two commas in a sentence—can make the meaning of the sentence very different. Remember that nonessential information should be set off by commas, and essential information should not be set off.

It is amazing how many people properly insert the first comma that sets off nonessential expressions, but fail to insert the second comma. This is absolutely unacceptable. Here are two examples.

"Col. John Smith, the officer in charge of this unit is giving the commands." **Incorrect.**

Since "Col. John Smith" is identified by name as the person being referred to in this sentence, "the officer in charge of this unit" is nonessential information and should be set off by commas. It is quite common, however, for people to commit the mistake that makes this sentence incorrect. The mistake is to include the first comma (after "Smith" and before "the"), but to omit the second comma (after "unit" and before "is"). This is unacceptable. If you include the first comma, as you should, it is essential that you also include the second one. The sentence needs to read, "Col. John Smith, the officer in charge of this unit, is giving the commands."

> "My boss at work, Mildred Brown is very compe-
> tent." **Incorrect.**

The subject of the sentence is "my boss at work." The fact that her name is Mildred Brown is supplementary information. Therefore, "Mildred Brown" should be offset by commas. But, in this sentence, as was the case in the previous example, only the first comma (after "work" and before "Mildred") is included, and the second comma (between "Brown" and "is") is omitted. This is unacceptable. You must include both commas. It is amazing how many people make the mistake of including only the first comma. This sentence should read, "My boss at work, Mildred Brown, is very competent."

To recap, in deciding whether to use "that" or "which," we have learned the following:

✓ If it is information that is *essential* to the meaning of what is being said, you should use "that" without commas.

✓ If it is information that merely adds some supplementary or incidental information to something that has already been said, you should use "which" and set off the group of words with commas.

✓ Put another way, "that" is used to narrow or identify a particular item being referred to; "which" is used to add something about an item already identified.

✓ In referring to nonessential, supplementary expressions in general, all such expressions should be set off by commas.

In concluding this chapter, it is interesting to note that British writers and editors seldom make the distinction between using "that" or "which." But in the United States, making that distinction is an important emphasis of good grammar.

Chapter 6

Misusing the Apostrophe

Part A: Forming Plurals

There seems to be a lot of confusion about how to make nouns plural, especially the names of people. The primary misunderstanding focuses on the mistaken idea that the apostrophe is used in making nouns plural. This is not the case. The general rule is very simple:

- ✓ If a noun *does not* end in *s*, make it plural by adding *s*.

- ✓ If a noun *does* end in *s*, make it plural by adding *es*.

- ✓ One does not make a noun plural by using an apostrophe and an *s* ('s).

- ✓ The general rule in its entirety holds true for family names and proper nouns.

One of the most frequent errors in making a noun plural is adding an apostrophe and an *s* to the noun. This is especially true with family names. Regardless of what the "spelling and grammar" program on your computer indicates or what you have heard and seen used, I know of no time that you would use an apostrophe and an *s* to make a family name or proper noun plural.

Here are some examples of making family names plural that do *not* end in *s*.

> "The Smiths are going on vacation."
> **This is correct.**

But many people incorrectly make "Smith" plural by adding an apostrophe and an *s* (Smith's). Doing that is definitely incorrect. Remember the general rule. If a word does not end in *s*, make it plural by adding *s*. "Smith" does not end in *s*, so make it plural by adding *s* (Smiths).

> "The Kellys bought a new house." **This is correct.**

Since the singular of the name "Kelly" does not end in *s*, the plural is formed by adding *s* (Kellys).

> "The Harrisons drove to the grocery store this
> morning." **Correct.**

"Harrison" does not end in *s*, so the plural is formed by adding *s* (Harrisons).

Here are some examples of making family names plural that *do* end in *s*. Some of them may surprise you.

> "The Robertses are going on vacation."
> **This is correct.**

Again, remember the general rule. If the word ends in *s*, make it plural by adding *es*. Since "Roberts" ends in *s*, make it plural by adding *es* (Robertses).

> "The Jameses play bridge frequently." **Correct.**

Since "James" ends in *s*, the plural is formed by adding *es* (Jameses).

"The Joneses are having guests for dinner."
Correct.

Since "Jones" ends in *s*, the plural is formed by adding *es* (Joneses).

Although it is grammatically correct to add *es* to family names ending in *s* (Roberts, James, Jones, Bliss, Summers, and Wells, to name a few), it may appear somewhat cumbersome or clumsy. If you are not comfortable with using *es* to form the plural of a family name—not comfortable with the way it sounds or looks—simply reword the sentence, but do *not* add an apostrophe and an *s*. For example, consider the following:

"The Wellses are in New York this week." Reword the sentence and say, "The Wells family is in New York this week" or "Bill and Nancy Wells are in New York this week" or "Mr. and Mrs. Wells and their children are in New York this week."

There are some exceptions to the general rule that we are very familiar with, such as "children," the plural of "child"; "men," the plural of "man"; "women," the plural of "woman"; "babies," the plural of "baby"; "ladies," the plural of "lady"; "feet," the plural of "foot"; "mice," the plural of "mouse"; "leaves," the plural of "leaf"; "knives," the plural of "knife"; "oxen," the plural of "ox"; "deer" the plural of "deer"; and "sheep" the "plural of "sheep," to mention only a few of the more obvious ones.

There are, however, so many exceptions to the general rule of making nouns plural that we could not be expected to remember all of them. There are the irregular plural forms of nouns ending in *f*, *fe*, *o*, or *y*; the various plural forms of the many compound nouns that we use on a daily basis; and the unusual plural forms we use only occasionally, such as the plurals of abbreviations, academic degrees, and symbols, signs, numerals, and letters of the alphabet. There are the different ways of forming the plural of Native American tribes, depending on the tribe. The same holds for forming the plural of nationalities. And there are the plural nouns that are used in a singular sense.

One of the features in the bonus section of this book is an easy-to-use resource covering the irregular plural forms that most people will have need to use at one time or another (pages 100-112). The material is arranged in a format that makes it is easy to find the particular form that one is interested in, and most complicated questions about plurals will be answered.

If you end up being uncertain about the plural of a word, I suggest that you go to a good dictionary with a reputation for being thorough and reliable. People tend to assume that all dictionaries that use *Webster* in their titles qualify as reliable resources for grammar and spelling. That just is not the case! Many companies use the name "Webster" in the titles of their dictionaries, but such an inclusion does not guarantee scholarly quality or authenticity. Be certain that the dictionary you use is a reliable, scholarly resource for validating correct usages of grammar. I recommend the latest edition of *Merriam-Webster's Collegiate Dictionary*, as does *The Chicago Manual of Style*. Again, one needs to be careful. There are many dictionaries that include in their titles the word "college" or "collegiate."

If the word you are looking up has an irregular plural form, a good dictionary will include it. If more than one plural form is noted, you should use the first one listed. For unusual or very difficult plural forms, you may want to turn to *The Chicago Manual of Style*. But you will be very well served by remembering the simplicity of the general rule: if a noun does *not* end in *s*, make it plural by adding *s*; if a noun *does* end in *s*, make it plural by adding *es*. But do not make a noun or proper name plural by adding an apostrophe and an *s*.

Part B: Forming Possessives

A closely related subject to making nouns plural is the subject of forming the possessive case of both singular and plural nouns. The possessive case indicates ownership, belonging, possession, or relationship. Again, a primary problem seems to center on the

use of the apostrophe. The general rule for making nouns possessive is as follows:

✓ The possessive case of most singular nouns is formed by
adding an apostrophe and an *s* ('s).

✓ The possessive case of most plural nouns ending in *s* is
formed by adding only an apostrophe (').

✓ The possessive case of most plural nouns not ending in *s*
(usually referred to as irregular plurals) is formed by adding
an apostrophe and an *s*.

✓ This general rule holds true with family names and letters
used as a name.

Here are some examples of the correct formation of the possessive case for both singular and plural nouns. In considering the
singular and plural forms of the possessive case, it makes absolutely no difference how many things are being possessed. What
matters is whether the person or thing doing the possessing—the
possessor—is singular or plural.

"Robert Burns's poems represent some of the
best of eighteenth-century literature."

A singular noun (Burns) forms the possessive by adding an
apostrophe and an *s*. The fact that "poems" is plural is irrelevant.

"Charles's friends went to the ball game with him."

A singular noun (Charles) forms the possessive by adding an
apostrophe and an *s*. How many friends went with Charles is
unimportant.

"Bob Jones's car is in the garage."

A singular noun (Jones) forms the possessive by adding an apostrophe and an *s*.

"The Joneses' car is in the garage."

Plural of Jones. A plural noun ending in *s* (Joneses) forms the possessive by adding only an apostrophe ('). It makes no difference that only one car is being referred to.

"The dog's collar is leather."

There is only one dog. A singular noun (dog) forms the possessive by adding an apostrophe and an *s*.

"The dogs' collars are leather."

There are several dogs. A plural noun ending in *s* (dogs) forms the possessive by adding only an apostrophe. The number of collars being referred to is of no consequence.

"The puppies' paws are wet."

A plural noun ending in *s* (puppies) forms the possessive by adding only an apostrophe. The number of paws is irrelevant.

"The woman's department is located on the second floor."

A singular noun (woman) forms the possessive by adding an apostrophe and an *s*.

"The women's department is located on the second floor."

An irregular plural noun not ending in *s* (women) forms the possessive by adding an apostrophe and an *s*.

"The witch's brew is something to be avoided."

There is only one witch. A singular noun (witch) forms the possessive by adding an apostrophe and an *s*.

"The witches' brew is something to be avoided."

There are several witches. A plural noun ending in *s* (witches) forms the possessive by adding only an apostrophe.

"The child's toys need to be cleaned on a regular basis."

A singular noun (child) forms the possessive by adding an apostrophe and an *s*.

"The children's toys need to be cleaned on a regular basis."

An irregular plural noun not ending in *s* (children) forms the possessive by adding an apostrophe and an *s*. The number of toys is unimportant.

"The Smiths' marriage appears to be a lasting one."

Plural of Smith. Since the plural form of the family name Smith ends in *s* (Smiths), the possessive is formed by adding only an apostrophe.

"The Robertses' marriage appears to be a lasting one."

Plural of Roberts. The plural form of the family name Roberts ends in *s* (Robertses); therefore, the possessive is formed by adding only an apostrophe.

"FDR's first 100 days are used as a standard of comparison for current presidents."

Letters used in place of a name form the possessive using the general rule—singular possessive is formed by adding an apostrophe and an *s*. The number of days makes no difference.

"LBJ's political stories are legendary."

Letters used in place of a name form the possessive using the general rule—singular possessive is formed by adding an apostrophe and an *s*. The number of stories is immaterial.

"W's legacy is yet to be determined."

A letter used in place of a name forms the possessive using the general rule—singular possessive is formed by adding an apostrophe and an *s*.

The general rule for forming possessives also applies to letters, whether acronyms or initialisms, that are used as nouns. Here are some examples of correctly making possessives of such letters (abbreviations).

"A CEO's responsibilities continue to become more complex in today's business climate."

A singular abbreviation used as a noun forms the possessive by adding an apostrophe and an *s*. "CEO" becomes "CEO's."

"An RN's training is very important."

A singular abbreviation used as a noun forms the possessive by adding an apostrophe and an *s*. "RN" becomes "RN's."

"A VP's credentials should be adequate for assuming the responsibilities of the president."

Singular abbreviations used as a noun form the possessive by adding an apostrophe and an *s*. "VP" becomes "VP's."

"AAUP's officers are full-time employees."

AAUP is the abbreviation for the American Association of University Professors. It makes no difference that there are many professors in the association. It is one association. It makes no difference that "officers" is plural. AAUP is singular. The general rule applies. Make the singular possessive by adding an apostrophe and an *s*. "AAUP" becomes "AAUP's."

Before leaving the formation of possessives, we need to address the formation of the possessive case of personal and indefinite pronouns. A pronoun is a word that is used as a substitute for a noun. There are six classes or kinds of pronouns, but we are interested in only two: personal pronouns (sometimes referred to as definite pronouns) and indefinite pronouns.

Personal pronouns refer to a definite person or thing that has already been identified, and there is no question what noun is being referred to. Indefinite pronouns refer *in general* to people or things, not to specific people or things.

First, let's take a look at personal pronouns. There are very few of them. The following chart shows the *base form* (singular and plural) of all personal pronouns in the English language and their *possessive forms*.

	Singular		**Plural**	
	Base form of pronoun	Possessive form of pronoun	Base form of pronoun	Possessive form of pronoun
First person:	I	my, mine	we	our, ours
Second person:	You	your, yours	you	your, yours
Third person:	he, she, it	his, her, hers, its	they	their, theirs

Here are examples of each of the above possessive pronouns used in a sentence.

"Give me *my* hat."	"That hat is *mine*."
"Here are *your* gloves."	"Are you sure those are *yours*?"
"That is *his* car."	"*Her* car is blue."
"The dog is *hers*."	"*Its* paws are wet."
"*Our* house is down the street."	"That house is *ours*."
"The furniture in *your* house is new."	"The furniture is *yours* to use."
"*Their* bicycles are new."	"The bicycles are *theirs*."

Personal pronouns never use an apostrophe or an apostrophe and an *s* to form the possessive case. Never! Never! Never! The possessive forms of personal pronouns are never changed or added to. They remain as they are in the chart above. The most common mistake people make with possessive pronouns is inserting an apostrophe in possessive personal pronouns ending in an *s*—changing "its" to "it's," "hers" to "her's," "yours" to "your's," "ours" to "our's," and "theirs" to "their's." *Do not do this!*

Let's take, for example, changing "its" to "it's" in an attempt to form the possessive case. Doing this changes the entire meaning of a sentence. "It's" is a contraction for "it is," rather than indicating the possessive case. See the following examples of using "it's" and "its."

"*It's* a pretty dog, but *its* paws are dirty." **Correct.**

"*It's* a big car, but *its* motor is not powerful enough." **Correct.**

"*It's* a pretty suit, and *its* color really looks good on me." **Correct.**

Never use an apostrophe when forming the possessive case of a personal (definite) pronoun.

Now let's look at the possessive case of indefinite pronouns. Indefinite pronouns do not refer to any specific person or thing or to any specific group of persons or things, as personal pronouns do. Instead, indefinite pronouns refer *in general* to people or things. Unlike the personal pronouns, there are many indefinite pronouns. Examples of indefinite pronouns that are frequently used are "one," "each," "either," "everyone," "everybody," "everything," "someone," "somebody," "nobody," "anybody," "anyone," and "no one."

There is one primary difference in forming the possessive case of indefinite pronouns and in forming the possessive case of personal pronouns. The possessive case of indefinite pronouns is formed by adding an apostrophe and an *s*. Here are some correct examples.

"The constitution protects *one's* rights."

"*Anybody's* house could be destroyed by the storm."

"*Everyone's* dogs should be well cared for."

"Squirrels could bury nuts in *anyone's* yard."

> "*Nobody's* safety should be compromised."

> "*Everybody's* arguments should be considered."

Sometimes the adverb "else" will be used with the indefinite pronoun to express possession. In such cases, add an apostrophe and an *s* to "else," but not to the pronoun. Here are some examples.

> "This is somebody else's umbrella."

> "Do not interfere in someone else's business."

> "No one else's house was broken into."

> "Everyone else's schools were painted."

To recap, in this part of the chapter, we looked at rules for forming the possessive case for nouns and pronouns. The rules are as follows:

Nouns

- ✓ The possessive case of most singular nouns is formed by adding an apostrophe and an *s*.
- ✓ The possessive case of most plural nouns ending in *s* is formed by adding only an apostrophe.
- ✓ The possessive case of most plural nouns *not* ending in *s* (usually referred to as irregular plurals) is formed by adding an apostrophe and an *s*.
- ✓ These rules hold true with family names and letters used as a name.

Pronouns

✓ Personal pronouns use no apostrophe to form the possessive case.

✓ Indefinite pronouns add an apostrophe and an *s* to form the possessive case.

For easy reference, one of the features in the bonus section of this book discusses many irregular and special practices of forming the possessive case of nouns and pronouns that you may use frequently or only now and then (pages 112-127). In most cases, the possessive case for nouns and pronouns is formed by adhering to the general rules. There are, however, numerous instances that will be much better understood by turning to this bonus feature.

Chapter 7

Troublesome Verbs—"Lie," "Lay," "Laid," "Lain"

Many times I hear someone say to his or her dog, "Lay down." The dog does not do it. So the person goes on and says, "I just don't understand why my dog doesn't mind me." I want to say, "Because you are asking it to do the wrong thing. You should be asking your dog to *lie* down, not *lay* down. No wonder it doesn't know what to do."

Joking aside, the tenses of some verbs are irregular and confusing. The verb "to lie" (recline) is such a verb. It is frequently confused with the verb "to lay" (put or place). Let's sort this out.

The verb "lie" refers to one's reclining on a bed, on a couch, in a chair, on the floor, or reclining anyplace. It is something that you do for yourself—someone else does not do it to you or for you. If you ask your dog to lie down, it is something you are asking the dog to do for itself. "Lie" also can be used to indicate one's staying in a horizontal position.

The verb "lay" refers to one's placing, setting, or putting an object someplace. If you lay something down, it is something you are doing to or for somebody or something other than yourself. You are placing or setting something other than yourself on something. You do not lay yourself down on the bed; you would, instead, lie down on the bed. But if you were putting someone else in bed, you would lay or place that person on the bed.

The principal parts of any verb in the English language are (1) the present tense, (2) the past tense, and (3) the past participle. Let us look at the principal parts of the verbs "lie" and "lay."

Principal parts of lie (meaning to recline)	Principal parts of lay (meaning to put, place, or set down)
Present tense: lie	Present tense: lay
Past tense: lay	Past tense: laid
Past Participle: lain	Past participle: laid

If you have difficulty in deciding whether to use "lie" or "lay" in a sentence, instead of using "lie" or "lay," use the word "place." If it sounds all right to use "place," then the correct word to use is "lay"; if it does not sound all right to use "place," you should use "lie." Again, we are focusing on developing good listening skills. Here are examples of the present tense of both "lie" (recline) and "lay" (put or place) being used—incorrectly and correctly.

> "I plan to lay down and take a nap this afternoon."
> **Incorrect.**

The verb "lay" should be used only when referring to something a person is doing to or for someone or something other than himself or herself. The verb "lie" should be used when someone is doing something to and for himself or herself, as is the case in this sentence. Using the "place" test mentioned in the previous paragraph also lets you hear that "lay" is incorrect in this sentence. You do not need to learn a bunch of grammatical rules to know that it does not sound right to say, "I plan to place down and take a nap this afternoon." Your ear clearly tells you that the sentence should be: "I plan to *lie* down and take a nap this afternoon."

> "I will carry my baby to her bedroom and *lay* her in her crib."

Correct—something I am doing to and for someone else, not to myself. Also, the "place" test will enable your ear to let you hear that in this sentence it would be all right to use "place" instead of "lay," that is, to say, "…and place her in her crib."

"Please *lay* the books on the table."

Correct—something you are being asked to do to something else—to the books, not to yourself. Again, the "place" test enables you to hear that "lay" is correct in this sentence. It would be all right to say, "Please place the books on the table."

"Will you please tell your dog to *lie* down and stop barking?"

Correct—The dog is being told to do something to and for itself (to lie down), not something you are doing to or for the dog. Using the "place" test, you will hear that it does not work to say "…tell your dog to place down…" Hence, "lay" would be the wrong word. "Lie" is correct.

"Please lay down and rest before you drop dead."

Incorrect—the verb "lay" should be used only when referring to something you are doing to or for someone or something other than yourself. Again, using the "place" test enables your ear to tell you that "place" would not work here; you would never say, "Please place down and rest…" "Lay" is clearly the wrong verb. The correct form of the sentence is "Please *lie* down and rest before you drop dead." The sentence talks about something one is doing for himself or herself.

"Sometimes I *lie* in bed and watch television."

Correct—something I am doing, not something someone else is doing to or for me. The "place" test also enables you to hear that using "lay" in this sentence would be incorrect. You obviously would not say, "Sometimes I place in bed and watch television." "Lay" would be incorrect; "lie" is correct in this sentence.

Now let's look at examples of the past tense of both "lie" and "lay" being used correctly and incorrectly. People frequently get these wrong. Part of the confusion is that the past tense of "lie" is "lay," the same word as the base form or present tense of "lay," and part of the mix-up comes from not knowing whether to use the past tense of the verb "lie" or the past tense of the verb "lay." To make the correct choice, one needs to do three things: (1) be certain what the principal parts of "lie" and "lay" are; (2) remember that lie pertains to people doing something for themselves, and "lay" pertains to doing something for someone or something other than one's self; and (3) if you are uncertain, use the "place" test.

> "I laid down on the bed earlier this afternoon and took a nap."

Incorrect—this is the mistake many people make: using the past tense of "lay" (laid) when they should use the past tense of "lie" (lay). This is something I did to and for myself; therefore, it requires the past tense of "lie." Furthermore, "placed down" does not work here. The sentence should be "I *lay* down on the bed earlier this afternoon and took a nap." It is really important to remember that the past tense of "lie" is "lay" and the past tense of "lay" is "laid."

> "I *laid* my daughter on the bed so she could take a nap."

Correct—past tense of "lay" (to set, put down, or place), something I did to and for someone else. Also, "placed" could be used instead of "laid" in this sentence.

"My dog *lay* on his bed all this morning."

Correct—past tense of "lie" (recline), something the dog did to and for itself. "Placed" does not work here.

"I *laid* the books on the table earlier today."

Correct—past tense of "lay" (to set, put down, or place), something I did to something other than myself. "Placed" works in this sentence.

Now let's look at the past participle of "lie" and "lay." The past participle and the past tense of the great majority of verbs are the same. That is the case with the verb "lay." But there are some irregular verbs for which the past tense and past participle are different. The verb "lie" is such a verb, and people frequently get the past participle of "lie" wrong. Once again, one needs to focus on three things: (1) knowing what the principal parts of "lie" and "lay" are; (2) remembering that "lie" pertains to people doing something for themselves, and "lay" pertains to doing something for someone or something other than one's self; and (3) using the "place" test. Here are examples of the past participle of both "lie" and "lay" being used correctly.

"The books, having been *laid* on the table a week ago, are covered with dust."

Correct—past participle of "lay," something done to the books, not something the books did to or for themselves. Also, using "placed" instead of "laid" works.

"By tomorrow the books will have *lain* on the table for eight days."

Correct—this is a tricky one. The past participle of "lie" is used here because the sentence refers to what has been happening to the books after they were placed on the table—they continue to "lie" (remain) on the table after they were "laid" (placed) on the table several days ago. Using "placed" instead of "lain" does not work.

"Having *lain* in bed all afternoon, I feel rested this evening."

Correct—past participle of "lie," something I have done to and for myself, not something someone else has done to or for me. "Placed" does not work.

"Having *laid* my dog on his bed, he has *lain* there quietly for two hours."

Correct—in the first half of the sentence, the past participle of "lay" is used because it refers to something I did to and for the dog; in the second half of the sentence, the past participle of "lie" is used because it refers to something the dog continues doing for itself after having been placed on the bed earlier by someone else. "Placed" can be substituted for "laid," but not for "lain."

"I feel as if I could have *lain* in bed for a week."

Correct—the past participle of "lie" is used because the sentence refers to staying in a horizontal position, something I could have been doing for myself, not something someone else could have been doing to or for me. Also, "placed" does not work in this sentence.

To recap, in this chapter we have focused on the three principal parts of two verbs: "lay" (a regular verb) and "lie" (an irregular verb). When using "lie" and "lay," you need to remember the following:

- ✓ "Lie" is used when referring to something one is doing to or for himself or herself.

- ✓ "Lay" is used when referring to something that one is doing to or for someone or something other than himself or herself.

- ✓ In order to be consistently correct in using "lie" and "lay," it is necessary to have a working knowledge of the principal parts of "lie" and "lay."

- ✓ It is helpful (though not necessary) to use the "place" test in determining whether to use "lie" or "lay."

There are many other verbs that are troublesome for people, sometimes because the meaning of the verb is not understood, and sometimes because the principal parts of the verb are irregular. In this chapter we addressed only "lie" and "lay" because they are so frequently misused. However, for easy reference, the final bonus feature, "Principal Parts of Verbs Made Easy" (pages 129-135), is comprised of a long list of verbs and their principal parts. The list consists of both regular and irregular verbs. Many of the irregular verbs are well known, but many others are not and cause confusion. In some instances only one or two of the principal parts are well known. No one, not even the experienced grammarian, is expected to remember all of these. I keep a list of the principal parts of verbs in a drawer next to my computer and refer to it frequently. When you are in doubt about one of the principal parts of a verb, this final bonus feature will prove to be a quick and easy reference you can turn to for clarification.

Postscript to this chapter: To "lie" also means "to make a false statement with the intent to deceive." When using "lie" with this meaning, the verb becomes regular, and its principal parts are "lie," "lied," "lied."

Chapter 8

"Less" or "Fewer"

E xcept in mathematical equations where numbers are defined as being "less than" or "greater than" other numbers, "less" is used to refer to bulk or to a quantity, and "fewer" is used to refer to individual items or to a number, to something that can be counted. Here are some examples.

> "My new car uses fewer gallons of gasoline than my old one." **Correct.**

"Fewer" is correct because in this sentence "fewer" refers to "gallons," to individual units that can counted.

> "My new car uses less gasoline than my old one."
> **Correct.**

"Less" is correct because in this sentence "less" refers to bulk or quantity. "Less gasoline" is not a number or individual unit that can be counted.

> "Our new stove uses less electricity than our old one." **Correct.**

"Less electricity" is not an individual unit that can be counted, but a quantity.

> "Our new stove uses fewer kilowatt-hours than our old one." **Correct.**

"Fewer," instead of "less," is used in this sentence because "kilowatt-hours" are individual units that can be counted.

> "Express Lane—Less than 15 items." (This is frequently seen in grocery stores.) **Incorrect.**

Fifteen is a specific number that can be counted. "Less" should be used only with quantities that cannot be counted, not with specific numbers of items that can be counted.

> "Express Lane—Fewer than 15 items." **Correct.**

"Fewer" is used because it refers to fifteen items, a specific number of individual units that can be counted.

> "I have fewer customers this year and less money." **Correct.**

In this sentence, "fewer" refers to individual units that can be counted, and "less" refers to money in general—to an indefinite quantity that cannot be counted.

> "Fewer than fifteen applicants responded to the advertisement." **Correct.**

"Fewer" refers to individual units, to a specific number of people that can be counted.

> "I have less money in my pocket today." **Correct.**

In this sentence, "less" refers to an indefinite sum of money that cannot be counted.

> "I have fewer than twenty-five one-dollar bills in my pocket." **Correct.**

"Fewer" refers to a specific number of dollar bills, to individual units that can be counted.

Most grocery stores incorrectly use "less" in defining the number of items that may be checked out in an express lane. Recently I was at a grocery store that correctly used "fewer" in its express-checkout signs. I complimented the checkout clerk on the correct usage of "fewer" instead of "less." She looked a little puzzled, so I took about thirty seconds to tell her that most signs of this nature are incorrect and why, again complementing her on her store's correctness. She thanked me, but I knew she had no idea what I was talking about.

Here is a recap of the chapter:

✓ "Less" is used to refer to bulk or to a quantity.

✓ "Fewer" is used to refer to individual items or to a number, to something that can be counted.

Knowing the difference between the correct usages of "less" and "fewer" may seem to be of minor consequence. Don't be fooled! This is a distinction that, when used, definitely clarifies comparisons and makes what one says more compelling. If you are consistent in making this distinction when speaking and writing, others may not know exactly why, but they will look to you as one who makes comparisons with great clarity, and your points of view will be better understood and more likely to prevail.

Chapter 9

Commas and Semicolons in a Series

There are two types of series: the simple series and the complex series. We'll start by focusing on the simple series, and as we progress in our discussion, you'll understand the difference between the two types of series.

The general rule for a simple series is as follows:

✓ Elements in a series of three or more normally are separated by commas.

✓ The final two elements in the series should be joined by a conjunction (usually "and" or "or").

✓ A comma, called the "serial comma," should always be used before the conjunction joining the final two elements of the series.

Let's look at examples of the general rule being adhered to in simple series.

> "The morning is cool, crisp, and windy." Be sure to insert a comma before "and"—the conjunction joining the final two elements of the series.

"The dress comes in different colors: brown, black, blue, and pink." Be sure to insert a comma before "and"—the conjunction joining the final two elements of the series.

"You could get there by taking the bus, riding on a train, flying in an airplane, or driving your own car." Be sure to insert a comma before "or."

"He was tall, thin, and handsome." Be sure to include a comma before "and."

"Alice was working, Jane was sleeping, and Karen was planning what should be done next." Be sure to insert a comma before "and."

I emphasize using the serial comma because so many people fail to do this. The serial comma should *always* be included. Most authorities on grammar recommend including the serial comma. *The Associated Press Stylebook* is the only major stylebook or manual I know of that recommends *not* including a comma before the conjunction joining the final two elements of a simple series, but to include the serial comma only in a complex series. I have always wondered why this is. The only thing I can figure out is that newsprint media are always looking for ways to conserve space. But whatever the reason, all other well-grounded grammar books and stylebooks I am aware of call for placing a comma (or a semicolon in a complex series) before the conjunction joining the final two elements of a series of three or more. This is a practice everyone should adhere to, when writing for formal or informal purposes or for personal or business purposes—in other words, a practice that should always be followed.

The next examples are a little tricky. They also relate to inserting a comma before a conjunction joining the final two elements of a series. But be careful not to confuse this conjunction with an "or" or an "and" or an "ampersand" ("&," the symbol used for "and") that is found within the element itself. See the following examples.

> "The menu consisted of appetizers, soup or salad, the main course, dessert, and coffee or tea."

"Soup or salad" is the second element of the five-element series. The "or" in "soup or salad" is an internal part of the second element of the series and should not be preceded by a comma. The "or" in "coffee or tea" is an internal part of the fifth element of the five-element series, is not the conjunction joining the final two elements of the series, and should not be preceded by a comma. However, the "and" between "dessert" and "coffee" is a conjunction used to introduce the final element of the five-element series and should be preceded by a comma.

> "For breakfast they had bacon and eggs, toast and jelly, and coffee or tea."

Each of the first two elements ("bacon and eggs" and "toast and jelly") of the three-element series has an internal "and," and the final element ("coffee or tea") of the series has an internal "or." These should not be preceded by a comma. Only the final "and" of the sentence, which is the conjunction that introduces the final element of the series, should be preceded by a comma.

> "John was working in the garden, Mary was working in the house, and the children were playing and eating candy bars."

Only the first "and" in the sentence is preceded by a comma. It is the conjunction that introduces the final element of the series. The second "and" in the sentence is an internal part of the third and final element of the series.

"The following four educational institutions are
located in Virginia: Randolph-Macon College, College of William and Mary, Johnson & Wales University, and Washington and Lee University."

Be sure to insert a comma only before the conjunction that
joins the final two elements of the series—the conjunction that
comes immediately prior to Washington and Lee University.

An exception to the general rule about using commas between
the elements of a series is that no comma is needed to separate the
elements of a series if all of the elements in the series are joined by conjunctions (either the same or different conjunctions). For example,

"I am not certain whether the pep rally is at the
high school or at the field house or at the civic hall."

All three elements are connected by the conjunction "or." No
commas are used to separate the elements of the series.

"Turn right at the corner and go two blocks and
turn left at the stop light and you will be there."

All four elements of the series are connected by "and," a conjunction. No commas are used.

"I got mad and said some things I shouldn't have and
need to apologize or everyone will think I am a jerk."

No commas are needed because all of the elements of the
series are connected by conjunctions.

I am not suggesting that connecting all the elements of a
series with a conjunction is a style of grammar I recommend. In
most instances it is *not* a construction that I am fond of because
without commas as guides, the elements of the series can take
longer to recognize and separate as you read. What I am saying
is that if you want to use that technique *occasionally*, it is gram-

matically correct as long as you do not separate the elements of the series with commas.

Thus far we have addressed rules and standards of grammar for a simple series. There are also rules and standards for the punctuation of a complex series of three or more.

✓ If the individual elements of a series involve internal punctuation, or when the elements of a series are unusually long or complex, the elements of the series should be separated by semicolons instead of by commas.

✓ It is up to the writer to decide whether or not to include a conjunction between the final two elements of the series— it is, so to say, a fielder's choice (although not absolutely essential, for clarity purposes in most instances including the conjunction is highly recommended).

✓ If the conjunction is included, it must be preceded by a semicolon rather than a serial comma.

Here are some examples of correct punctuation for a complex series.

> "Mr. Johnson drives a Cadillac, which is black and has large, silver wheels; Mrs. Johnson drives a Lexus, which is silver and has regular wheels and tires; and their son, James, drives a Jeep Grand Cherokee, which is dark red and has oversized wheels and tires."

Each element of the series is a sentence in itself and has internal punctuation. Therefore, semicolons instead of commas are used to separate the individual elements of this series. Also, note that the final element (referring to the son's car) is immediately preceded by a conjunction ("and"). When a conjunction is used to connect the final two elements of a complex series, a semicolon must be used prior to that conjunction.

"James is a young artist who specializes in outdoor scenes; Alice, his sister, also paints, but concentrates on indoor scenes; and Thomas, the youngest member of the family, has little interest in artistic matters and devotes his time to playing golf."

Each element of the series is a sentence in itself and has internal punctuation. The elements of the series are, therefore, separated by semicolons. The conjunction ("and") connecting the second and third elements of the series is preceded by a semicolon.

"During the rain, the most experienced of the hunters remained in the tent with the camping equipment and stayed dry; another camper slept in his sleeping bag outside the tent, but by morning was soaked; and a third camper stayed dry by sleeping in the cab of the pickup truck."

The elements in this series are separated by semicolons because they are complex and have internal punctuation. The conjunction ("and") separating the second and third elements is preceded by a semicolon.

Names of companies, professional firms, and partnerships

With the names of companies, professional firms, partnerships, and so forth, the customary rules and standards for grammar are generally different from those applied to the regular simple series. These differences include the following:

✓ The serial comma (the comma before the conjunction connecting the final two elements in a series of three or more) is usually omitted in a company name. This is the case whether the word "and" appears in the name or the ampersand (&) is used instead of "and." (The use of an ampersand is not recommended for the general text of written material, and its use in a series is primarily found in the names of companies or professional firms.)

✓ Many times the "and" connecting the final two names in a series of three or more is omitted.

✓ Occasionally no commas will be used to separate the names in a series. When this is the case, "and" will definitely not be used to join the final two names of the series, and the number of names in the series will usually be limited to not fewer than three or more than five (however, I have seen only two names used in this way).

Let's look at examples of several names of companies and professional firms.

"Quinn, Franklin & Brown, LLC, Attorneys at Law" (no comma before "&")

"Jackson, Jackson & Jackson, Family Hardware" (no comma before "&")

"Johnson, Miller and Anderson, Medical Doctors" (no comma before "and")

"Peters, Blakedale and Peters, Inc." (no comma before "and")

"Sandberg, Sandberg, Goldmann, CPAs" ("and" omitted)

"Jackson, Finch, Smith, PC, Doctors of Medical Dentistry" ("and" omitted)

"Blanchard Blanchard Blanchard, Attorneys at Law" (no commas)

"Carter Nelson Fields Hoffman Newman, PC, Medical Clinic" (no commas)

When dealing with the names of companies and professional firms, one can never be certain what exceptions to the general rules and standards of grammar have been utilized. If you do not want to be embarrassed, be sure to do your homework before engaging in correspondence with a company or professional firm. Most companies and professional firms today have websites. There is little excuse for not knowing the exact name of a company or professional firm before contacting it.

Commas with addresses and dates

There are special rules for the use of commas separating the elements of two other kinds of series: addresses and dates. When including the name of a town or city with the name of the state, a comma is used before and after the state. With the month-day-year style of dates, commonly used in the United States, a comma should be placed before and after the year, as in the following examples.

> "New train service between St. Louis, Missouri, and Chicago, Illinois, will start on October 1, 2010, and will continue as long as the demand justifies the cost to the states."

> "Abraham Lincoln was born on February 12, 1809, near Hodgenville, Kentucky, to Thomas Lincoln and Mary Hanks."

The mistake most frequently made with both addresses and dates is similar: including the comma separating the town or city from the state, but omitting the comma after the state, and including the comma that separates the date in the month from the year, but omitting the comma after the year. Commas must be included *before and after the state* following a town and *before and after the year* following the date in a month. If the state or year comes at the end of the sentence, then a period instead of a comma would be used following the state or year.

> "Abraham Lincoln was born on February 12, 1809,
> near Hodgenville, Kentucky."

> "The graduation dance was in St. Louis, Missouri,
> on May 15, 2009."

No commas are used when only a city is named without including the state or a state is mentioned without including a city. Likewise, no commas are use when only a month and date in the month are used without including the year, or when only a month and year are used without including the date of the month.

> "New train service between St. Louis and Chicago
> will start on October 1 and will continue as long as
> the demand justifies the cost."

> "The new train service between Missouri and Il-
> linois will start in October 2010 and will continue
> as long as the demand justifies the cost to the two
> states."

> "Abraham Lincoln served as president from March
> 1861 until April 1865."

With the day-month-year system, commonly used in the military and some research documents, but not usually in regular text, no commas are used.

> "Orders for 1 April 2010 call for all planes, ships,
> and ground forces to attack predesignated targets."

> "Historians will, no doubt, check the e-mails and
> written orders between commanders dated 1 April
> 2010."

Let's recap this chapter.

In a simple series of three or more elements

✓ the elements are normally separated by commas;

✓ the final two elements in the series should be joined by a conjunction (usually "and" or "or");

✓ a comma, called the "serial comma," should always be used before the conjunction joining the final two elements of the series.

In a complex or complicated series

✓ the elements of the series should be separated by semicolons instead of by commas;

✓ although it is not essential, in most instances it is helpful to connect the final two elements with a conjunction;

✓ if a conjunction is used, a semicolon should precede the conjunction;

✓ companies and professional firms usually use a different set of grammatical standards;

✓ there are special rules for using commas with addresses and dates.

Chapter 10

Commas between Adjectives

Knowing when to put commas between adjectives seems to cause people a great deal of trouble. But it shouldn't. The general rule is quite simple:

✓ When a noun is preceded by two or more adjectives, a comma separates the adjectives if they are equal in rank (if the adjectives modify the noun in the same way or to the same degree, they are considered equal in rank).

✓ If the adjectives are not equal in rank, no comma is used.

When you are not certain whether or not the adjectives are equal in rank, there is an easy way to make that determination. If the comma between two adjectives can be replaced with the word "and" without changing the meaning of what is being said, the adjectives are equal in rank and require being separated by a comma.

Here are examples of adjectives that are equal in rank. They modify the noun in the same way and require a comma separating them.

"The long, hot summer days cause one to be lazy."

The summer days are both long and hot. "Long" and "hot" modify "summer days" in the same way and are, therefore, equal in rank. A comma is required. If you are in doubt about this, apply the "and" test. Can the comma between "long" and "hot" be replaced with the word "and" without changing the meaning of the sentence? The answer is yes! One could say, "The long and hot summer days cause one to be lazy." There is no question about it—the comma is required. "Long" and "hot" are equals—they modify "summer days" in the same way.

"The ripe, juicy apple is really good to eat."

The apple is both ripe and juicy. "Ripe" and "juicy" modify "apple" in the same way and are, therefore, equal in rank. The comma is required. If you are in doubt about this, apply the "and" test. Can the comma between "ripe" and "juicy" be replaced with "and" without changing the meaning of the sentence? Yes. One could say, "The ripe and juicy apple is really good to eat."

"Bill is a pleasant, loyal friend."

The comma between "pleasant" and "loyal" can be replaced with "and." One could say, "Bill is a pleasant and loyal friend." "Pleasant" and "loyal" are equal in rank. The comma is needed.

"She told her children not to play in the dark, deserted alley."

The comma between "dark" and "deserted" can be replaced with "and." The sentence could read "…in the dark and deserted alley." Both "dark" and "deserted" modify "alley" in the same way. "Dark" and "deserted" are equals. The comma is needed.

Here are examples of adjectives that are *not* equal in rank—that is, do not modify the noun in the same way. Therefore, separating them with a comma would be incorrect.

"At bedtime she told the children a quiet short story."

In this sentence, "quiet" and "short" are not used in the same way and, therefore, are not equal in rank. "Short" and "story" belong together as a unit; she told her children a short story. The short story was a quiet one. "Quiet" stands alone and modifies "short story." A comma is not used to separate "quiet" and "short." If you are not certain, apply the "and" test. Without changing the meaning of the sentence, could you say, "At bedtime she told the children a quiet and short story"? The answer is no. A story that is short and a short story are not quite the same thing. "Quiet" and "short" are not equals, and no comma should be used to separate them.

"He believes in attending traditional religious services."

In this sentence, "traditional" and "religious" are not used in the same way and, therefore, are not equals. "Traditional" refers to the kind of religious services he believes in attending. Using the "and" test, one would not say, "He believes in attending traditional and religious services." No comma is used.

"She sleeps with her young black cat."

She sleeps with her black cat. Her black cat happens to be young. "Black" and "young" are not equal in rank. One would not say, "She sleeps with her young and black cat." No comma is used.

"The old stone wall is built of native stones taken from the fields."

"Old" and "stone" are not equal. The sentence refers to a stone wall that happens to be old. One would not say, "The old and stone wall…" No comma is used.

To recap, the general rule for putting commas between adjectives is as follows:

✓ When a noun is preceded by two or more adjectives, a comma separates the adjectives if they are equal in rank.

✓ If the adjectives are not equal in rank, no comma is used.

Deciding whether or not to place a comma between two adjectives should be one of the easiest grammatical decisions to make. The general rule is quite simple, and there are no exceptions to the rule. Furthermore, using the "and" test should eliminate any question about the matter.

Summary

There are many other important subjects relating to the correct usage of grammar that could be addressed. However, this book is not meant to be a complete guide to grammar. It is, instead, meant to call attention to some of the most frequently made grammatical mistakes, how to recognize them, and how to fix them.

Am I the final authority? Of course not. Other writers may disagree with my selection of the most frequently made grammatical errors. There will be those who disagree with the order in which I have arranged the chapters. Some grammarians may find fault with my playing down the necessity of learning parts of speech and rules of grammar. But I guarantee that if you master the subjects dealt with in the pimary chapters of this book, which should not be all that difficult, and acquaint yourself with the bonus section and the appendix, you will stand out as being well versed in grammar.

In recapping, the following concerns are addressed in the introduction and each of the chapters.

Introduction: There are ten errors of grammar that many people make on a rather regular basis in their personal and professional lives. It is relatively easy to fix them. The introduction stresses the importance of learning how to listen to what you are saying in order to identify and correct grammatical errors.

Chapter 1: The single most frequently made grammatical error, in the opinion of this writer, is the use of "I" instead of "me." The problem occurs primarily when using "I" or "me" with another person's name. You can recognize and fix this problem without having to learn rules of grammar. Just delete the other person's name from the sentence, and you will usually *hear* whether to use "I" or "me." In some instances, it is necessary to complete the sentence in order to hear whether it is correct to use "I" or "me."

Chapter 2: The two ways we learned in chapter 1 to determine whether to use "I" or "me" also apply to deciding whether to use "he" or "him" or "she" or "her," especially with other names. Again, the need to listen is stressed.

Chapter 3: This chapter deals with the use of punctuation—the period, comma, semicolon, colon, question mark, and exclamation point—with quotation marks. Three specific rules are stressed: (1) commas and periods *always* precede closing quotation marks; (2) colons and semicolons *always* follow closing quotation marks; (3) question marks and exclamation points *always* follow closing quotation marks *unless* the question mark or exclamation point belongs to the material being quoted. These rules and standards are different in Great Britain.

Chapter 4: This chapter looks at the "ing" thing—at action words (referred to in grammar books as verbs) that have "ing" added to them. The general rule is, when an action word (a verb) ending in "ing" is preceded by a person's name or a personal pronoun and focuses on or modifies the act and not the actor, the name or personal pronoun should be in the possessive case. If, on the other hand, the action word ending in "ing" refers to or modifies the actor and not the act, the name or personal pronoun preceding the action word is not in the possessive case. If the *act* is emphasized, possessive form is used; if the *actor* is focused on, the possessive form is not used.

Chapter 5: This chapter explores when to use "which" and when to use "that." If it is information essential to the meaning of what is being said, "that" is used. If the information merely adds some supplementary information to something that has already been said, "which" is used. In other words, "that" is used to narrow or identify a particular item being referred to; "which" is used to add something about an item already identified. "Which" phrases or expressions—that is, nonessential information—are set off by commas.

Chapter 6: There seems to be a lot of confusion about the use of the apostrophe with making nouns plural and in forming the possessive case of nouns. In most instances a plural noun is not formed by using an apostrophe and an *s* ('s). The general rule for making a noun plural is that if the noun does not end in *s*, make it plural by adding *s*; if the noun ends in *s*, make it plural by adding *es*. This holds true for family names as well. There are some exceptions. Part B of the bonus section deals with various irregular plurals of nouns.

A closely related subject to making nouns plural is forming the possessive case of singular and plural nouns. Again, using the apostrophe correctly is crucial. The general rule is, the possessive case of most singular nouns is formed by adding an apostrophe and an *s*; the possessive of most plural nouns ending in *s* is formed by adding only an apostrophe ('); and the possessive case of most plural nouns not ending in *s* (usually referred to as irregular plurals) is formed by adding an apostrophe and an *s*. This general rule holds true with family names. Part C of the bonus section pertains to several irregular, special, and unusual particulars of forming the possessive case.

Chapter 7: The verb "lie" refers to one's reclining someplace. It is something that you do for yourself—someone else does not do it to you or for you. "Lie" also can be used to indicate staying in a horizontal position. The verb "lay" refers to one's placing an object(s) someplace. It is something that you do to or for someone or something other than yourself. The principal parts of the verb "lie" are "lie," "lay," "lain"; the principal parts of the verb "lay" are "lay," "laid," "laid."

Chapter 8: Except in mathematical equations where numbers are defined as being "less than" or "greater than" other numbers, "less" is used to refer to bulk or to a quantity, and "fewer" is used to refer to individual items or to a number, to something that can be counted.

Chapter 9: In a simple series, the individual elements of the series are separated by a comma, with the final two elements of the series being joined by a conjunction (usually "and" or "or") preceded by a comma. In a complex series, the individual elements are separated by semicolons instead of by commas. Complex company names and addresses and dates are also considered series and have special rules.

Chapter 10: When a noun is preceded by two or more adjectives, the adjectives are separated by a comma if they are equal in rank; if the adjectives are not equal, no comma is used. Adjectives are considered to be equal in rank when they modify the noun in the same way.

By spending the time needed to master the subjects addressed in the ten chapters of this book, you will become much more confident in your use of grammar and, as a result, will become a much stronger communicator. The bottom line is that you will be respected by yourself and others for who and what you are and for what you can become. You will be happier and more successful in your personal relationships and your professional endeavors. Paying attention to, and correcting, your grammar will reap meaningful and practical dividends for you in every area of your life.

The ten chapters of this book pertain to the types of grammatical situations most people deal with on a daily basis in both their personal and professional relationships. The two concluding entries of the book are also very important. The bonus section (pages 95-135), which follows immediately, is filled with all kinds of time-saving references that you will find very useful. The appendix (pages 137-143) deals with reminders of ten significant changes in grammatical standards that have taken place gradually over the past twenty-five to thirty years and that many people may not be aware of. Reviewing the appendix will keep you from the embarrassment of being out-of-date.

Bonus Section

Time-Saving References

This bonus section is included so the reader will have quick-and-easy references for understanding irregular and unusual grammatical practices that could take hours to research. Including these materials in the regular chapters of the book would have made the book unduly complex and unhandy.

Although most people will find it necessary to refer to these materials only occasionally, having them readily available at your fingertips when you do need them will save you hours of time and effort. Furthermore, having them available will give you the tools to be more versatile—to be more creative—in the ways you present your ideas or discuss your concerns. Having this special arsenal available will give you the added ammunition that leads to greater self-confidence and to becoming a more accomplished communicator.

Personally, I keep the materials in parts B, C, and D—which address exceptions to the general rules for forming plurals, irregular and special examples of forming possessives, and the principal parts of verbs—near my computer or in a top drawer of my desk so I can turn to them quickly. No one is expected to remember all of this information without some prompts.

William B. Bradshaw, PhD

Part A: All about "Who" or "Whom"

When I tell people what this book is about, almost without exception they reply something like this: "I bet using 'who' and 'whom' ranks right up toward the top of the list of grammatical errors." This indicates to me that there is much uncertainty about the correct usage of "who" and "whom." This concern, however, seems to be overrated.

I appear to be in the minority in this matter, because I favor keeping a clear distinction between when to use "who" and when to use "whom." But the trend in the United States is clearly toward *not* making such a distinction except in formal writing—that is, a trend toward using "who" most of the time. One reason for this is that even in formal writing, where the distinction is still adhered to, good grammar calls for "who" to be used much more frequently than "whom." It is interesting to note how often people who do not understand the difference between when to use "who" or "whom" overcompensate by using "whom" when "who" should have been used. If you are not certain whether to use "who" or "whom," there is no question about it—use "who." You are much more likely to be correct—formally as well as informally.

Then why have I included this short article on the correct usage of "who" and "whom" when the trend is toward not considering it a subject that should be included among the "big ten" of grammatical errors? There are two reasons: (1) so many people assume this *is* among the top ten grammatical errors that failure to include this material would cast doubts on the validity of the book, and (2) to demonstrate to those people like myself, who believe that keeping the distinction between "who" and "whom" leads to greater clarity and feel more comfortable with retaining those differences, how uncomplicated the entire topic really is, thus enabling them to use "who" and "whom" with certainty and confidence.

Here is all you need to concentrate on when using "who" or "whom," which refer only to human beings, not to other animals or things. "Who" should be used when referring to the person or persons doing that which is being done. Put another way, "who" refers to the person(s) of action. In grammatical terms I am referring to the subject of the verb, whether it is the subject of the verb in the main sentence or the subject of the verb in a secondary or supporting clause. If, on the other hand, the person(s) being referred to is not the person(s) doing that which is being done, "whom" is used. It is just that simple.

Let's look at some examples.

"Bill is the one who was driving the car."

"Who" is correct because it refers to the person of action, the person doing what was being done—that is, to Bill, who "was driving the car."

"Who is going to the movie tonight?"

"Who" is correct because it refers to the person or persons of action, the person(s) "going to the movie tonight."

"Alice, who was riding in the passenger seat, was injured."

There are two verbs in this sentence—two different things going on: "was riding" and "was injured." Pay attention only to the action that "who" refers to. "Who" is correct because it refers to the person of action—that is, to the person who "was riding in the passenger seat." Pay no attention to the parts of the sentence that tell us "Alice...was injured."

"Whom did you give the book to?"

"Whom" is correct because it does *not* refer to the person of action. "Whom" did not "give the book"; "whom" received the book. "Whom," therefore, is correct. If you rearrange the question, it becomes very clear that "you" is the person of action: "You gave the book to whom?"

"Who gave the books to whom?"

Both "who" and "whom" are used correctly in this sentence. "Who" is the person of action, the person who "gave the books." "Whom" is the person the books were given to. Since "whom" does not refer to the person or persons doing what is being done, it is correct to use "whom" instead of "who" at the end of the sentence.

"Who do you think called the police?"

Many people incorrectly use "whom" in this sentence. There are two verbs (words of action) in this sentence ("think" and "called") and two pronouns ("who" and "you"). To see clearly what the role of "who" is, just rearrange the words into this question: "You think who called the police?" When the sentence is rearranged, it is clear that "who" is correct because it refers to a person or persons of action, to the person who "called the police." "You" is also a person of action ("you think"), but how "you" is used is unimportant for our purpose of deciding whether "who" or "whom" should be used in this sentence.

"Regardless of what you think, I know whom I saw."

Many people incorrectly use "who" instead of "whom" in this situation. We are concerned only about the second part of this sentence: "I know whom I saw." "Whom" is correct because "whom" is not the person of action. "Whom" did not see; "I" saw, and "whom" was seen.

"Who" and "whom" can be made into compound pronouns by adding "ever." "Whoever" and "whomever" follow the same grammatical guidelines as do "who" and "whom." Let's look at some examples.

"I am grateful to whoever called the police."

Whoever is correct because it refers to the person or persons of action, to the person doing what was being done—to the person who "called the police."

"I will buy a ticket for whoever wants to go to the movie with me."

Do not be confused because there is more than one thing that is being done. Do not worry about buying the ticket; concentrate on "wants to go." Whoever is correct because it refers to the person of action, to the person doing that which is being done in this part of the sentence—that is, to whoever "wants to go to the movie with me."

"I will buy a ticket for whomever I want to take with me to the movie."

In this sentence, there are two actions or two things going on: buying a ticket and wanting to take to the movie. "Whomever" refers to the second action—"want to take with me to the movie." "I" is the person of action, the person doing what is being done in this part of the sentence—that is, "I want to take…" "Whomever" is not the person doing the taking, but the person who is being taken to the movie. Therefore, "whomever" is correct.

"Please give a book to whoever comes into the store."

Again, there are two actions, two things going on: "give a book" and "comes into the store." "Whoever" refers to the second action—to "whoever comes into the store." Since "whoever" refers to the person of action, to the person doing what is being done, "whoever" is correct.

Let's recap this section:

- ✓ In the United States, the trend is toward not making a distinction between using "who" or "whom" except in formal writing.

- ✓ "Who" should be used when referring to the person or persons doing the action. If the person being referred to is not the person of action, not the person doing what is being done, "whom" is used.

- ✓ "Whoever" and "whomever" follow the same grammatical standards as "who" and "whom."

- ✓ If you do not know whether to use "who" or "whom" and you have to take a guess at it, the odds of your being correct definitely favor going with "who."

In the second paragraph of this article, I suggested that in the United States the trend is toward accepting the use of "who" in most instances other than in formal writing—that is, to just forgetting about using "whom" altogether. In Great Britain it is an entirely different matter. This article would be completely out of place. In Great Britain it would be expected that the classical distinction between when to use "who" and when to use "whom" would be strictly adhered to in all circumstances. Using "who" where "whom" should be used would be considered a major grammatical error in Great Britain—definitely among the "big ten" of errors.

Part B: Forming the Plural of Nouns: Special Exceptions to the Rules

There are basic rules for forming the plural of nouns. But there are also many exceptions to those rules. A good dictionary, therefore, is essential for checking the correct plural for nouns that form the plural in an unusual or irregular manner. If a dictionary does not include the plural of a particular noun, it means that the plural of that noun is generally known and does not need to be included in the dictionary. If the dictionary gives two different acceptable plural forms, the preferable form is the first one listed. Most authorities on grammar suggest that a Webster dictionary is preferable. There are, however, many different kinds of Webster dictionaries—some good and others not so good. I strongly recommend *Merriam-Webster's Collegiate Dictionary*.

Now let's look at basic rules for forming the plural of nouns and special exceptions to those rules.

Plural of ordinary nouns

The plural of most nouns is formed by adding *s* if the singular does not end in *s*, and *es* if the singular of the noun ends in *s* or in an "*s* sound" (*ch, j, s, sh, x,* or *z*; for example, "church" becomes "churches," "dress" becomes "dresses," "parish" becomes "parishes," "glass" becomes "glasses," "box" becomes "boxes," and "birch" becomes "birches"). Many nouns do not, however, fall into the category of being ordinary nouns and form their plurals in other ways.

Nouns ending in *f* or *fe*

Nouns ending in *f* or *fe* are treated differently. Some singular nouns ending in *f* or *fe* form the plural by adding an *s* (for example, "chief" becomes "chiefs," "dwarf" becomes "dwarfs," "roof" becomes "roofs," and "safe" becomes "safes"). Other singular nouns ending in *f* or *fe* form the plural by changing the *f* to *v* and adding *es* (for example, "loaf" becomes "loaves," "leaf" becomes "leaves," "knife" becomes "knives," and "wolf" becomes "wolves"). And the same singular noun may have one plural form in the United States (for example, "wharf" becomes "wharves") and another plural form in England ("wharf" becomes "wharfs"). If you do not know the correct plural form for a particular noun, turn to your dictionary.

Nouns ending in o

Nouns ending in *o* also form their plurals differently. Some nouns ending in *o* form the plural by adding *s* (for example, "piano" becomes "pianos," and "solo" becomes "solos"). Some nouns ending in *o*, on the other hand, form the plural by adding *es* ("hero" becomes "heroes," and "potato" becomes "potatoes"). Many singular nouns ending in *o* can form the plural by adding either s or es ("tuxedo" can become "tuxedos" or "tuxedoes," "cargo" can become "cargoes" or "cargos," and "volcano" can become "volcanoes" or "volcanos"). And yet other singular nouns ending in *o* are in a transitional phase and can become plural be adding either *s* or *es*, but one variant is definitely preferred over the other ("avocados" is preferred over "avocadoes" and "zeros" over "zeroes"). There are no firm rules for knowing whether to use *s* or *es* in making such nouns plural. The following guidelines and trends, however, are helpful, but keep in mind that they are only trends and guidelines, not rules.

If the final *o* is preceded by a vowel, the plural is usually formed by adding an *s*. If the final *o* is preceded by a consonant, the plural is frequently formed by adding *es*, but the trend is toward making such words plural by adding only an *s*. And the plural of a noun ending in *o* is usually formed by adding *s* to the singular in the following circumstances: if the noun has been borrowed from another language (for example, "bistro" becomes "bistros," and "casino" becomes "casinos"); if the noun is a proper name ("Alberto" becomes "Albertos," and "Fazio" becomes "Fazios"); or if the noun is a shortened form of a longer word ("photo" [shortened from photograph] becomes "photos"). There is little rhyme or reason to dealing with making nouns plural that end in *o*, and I strongly recommend that you keep that dictionary within easy reach!

Nouns ending in y

Nouns ending in *y* form the plural by following one of two rules. (1) If the singular noun is common and the ending *y* is preceded by *qu* or a consonant, change the *y* to *i* and add *es* (for example, "soliloquy" becomes "soliloquies," "berry" becomes "berries," "folly" becomes "follies," "ally" becomes "allies," "mummy" becomes "mummies," "lady" becomes "ladies," and "baby" becomes "babies"). (2) If the noun is proper or if the final *y* is preceded by a vowel, the plural is formed by adding *s* (for example, "Teddy" becomes "Teddys" [the Teddys of the world], "Henry" becomes "Henrys" [there are many Henrys in the world], "Mary" becomes Marys," "donkey" becomes "donkeys," "monkey" becomes "monkeys," "ploy" becomes "ploys," and "buoy" becomes "buoys.") An apostrophe is never used to form the plural of a family name (for example, "the Harrisons live here" [not the Harrison's], "the Jacksons own that car" [not the Jackson's], or "the Joneses have a new boat" [not the Jones's or Jones']).

Plural of Native American tribes

How to form the plural names of Native American tribes is in a transitional stage. In years past, the singular and plural were always the same. However, the trend now is shifting toward making tribal names plural by adding *s* to the singular (for example, "Cherokee" becomes "Cherokees," "Delaware" becomes "Delawares," "Hopi" becomes "Hopis," "Mohawk" becomes "Mohawks," and "Osage" becomes "Osages"). *The Chicago Manual of Style* suggests that the names of all Native American tribes are now made plural by adding *s*, whereas *Merriam-Webster's Collegiate Dictionary* normally prefers the singular and plural of Native American tribes to be the same and includes adding the *s* to form the plural as a "secondary variant" in most instances. Whenever we are going through a transitional change for correct grammatical usage, there will be confusion about what the correct form is. Currently, you would be correct to use either way for forming the plural of most tribal names. It is pretty clear, however, in what direction we are moving. In not too many years all authorities will probably agree that tribal names should be made plural by adding *s*.

Irregular plurals

Several nouns have irregular plurals. For example, "basis" becomes "bases," "ox" becomes "oxen," "child" becomes "children," "man" becomes "men," "woman" becomes "women," "brother" becomes either "brothers" or "brethren" ("brothers" is the preferred term, but either is currently considered correct), "foot" becomes "feet," "goose" becomes "geese," and "mouse" becomes "mice." Some nouns are the same whether singular or plural (for example, "chassis," "corps," "sheep," "moose," and "swine"). "Fish," "deer," "quail," and "grouse" are normally the same in singular and plural, but it may surprise you to know that *Merriam-Webster's Collegiate Dictionary* also permits the use of "fishes," "deers," "quails," and "grouses." And Webster says that "data," although strictly speaking the plural of "datum," is well established as both a singular and plural noun. Many irregular plural forms are well known; others are not. Again, a dictionary will come in handy.

Plurals of national group names

There are not many surprises in regard to the plural forms of inhabitants of countries. For example, many follow the general rule for making a singular noun plural by adding an *s*: "Roman," "Norman," "German," "African," "Cuban," "Russian," "Spaniard," "Canadian," and "American" become respectively "Romans," "Normans," "Germans," "Africans," "Cubans," "Russians," "Spaniards," "Canadians," and "Americans." Others adhere to a well-known irregular form: for example, "Dutchman" becomes "Dutchmen," "Englishman" becomes "Englishmen," "Frenchman" becomes "Frenchmen," "Irishman" becomes "Irishmen," and "Scotsman" becomes "Scotsmen." There are, however, some other differences. Some ethnic and national groups are the same whether singular or plural; for example, "Burmese," "Chinese," and "Japanese." And in some instances accepted practices of grammar permit us to use a singular noun in a plural sense in referring to an entire group or nation of people. For example, it is common to refer to "the British," "the Dutch," "the English," "the French," or "the Irish." Political correctness is currently much in the forefront, and I strongly suggest checking with Webster if you have any question about the correct plural form of national group names.

Plurals of compound nouns

Compound nouns, with or without hyphens, form the plural by making the principal word plural using the same ending for the principal word as when it is used alone as a plural, for example, "sons-in-law," "mothers-in-law," "commanders in chief," "attorneys general," "postmasters general," "presidents-elect," "courts martial," and "passersby." But the principal word is not always the first word of compound nouns. For example: "by-products," "major donors," "fund-raising specialists," "motion pictures," "assistant attorneys," "corporate counsels," "deputy sheriffs," "chief financial officers," and "major generals." Occasionally, both nouns of a compound noun will be made plural, for example, "menservants," "brothers in arms," "masters of arts," and "gentlemen farmers." And then there are plurals of measurements for which the main noun is not the word that is normally made plural, for example, "spoonfuls," "cupfuls," "bucketfuls," and "handfuls." Keep that dictionary close at hand!

Plurals of letters, signs, symbols, figures, and so forth used as nouns

Forming the plurals of letters, signs, symbols, figures, abbreviations, and numerals—used and referred to as nouns—gets quite involved. Some are made plural by adding only an *s*, and some are made plural by adding an apostrophe and an *s* ('s).

The following make the plural form by adding only an *s*:

✓ capital letters used as words (for example, the three Rs, the Oakland As, and the As and Bs on your report card);

✓ numerals used as nouns (the 1990s, 727s, and temperatures in the low 20s); and

✓ abbreviations of more than one letter that contain no *interior* periods (for example, IRAs, your ABCs, VIPs, IOUs, MAs, vols., and eds.). But there are exceptions to this rule (for example, pp. is the plural form of p. [page]; nn. is the plural form of n. [note]; and MSS is the plural form of MS [manuscript]). If you are in question, go to your dictionary.

The following make the plural form by adding an apostrophe and an *s*:

✓ lowercase letters (only one letter);

✓ figures;

✓ symbols;

✓ abbreviations with two or more interior periods; and

✓ abbreviations with a combination of capital and lowercase letters.

Here are examples, all of which are correct, of the plurals of letters, signs, symbols, and so forth used and referred to as nouns:

"Mind your p's and q's, dot your i's, and cross your t's." (lowercase letters)

"I need a word with two e's and three s's." (lowercase letters)

"His *q*'s look like 8's, but not like $'s." (lowercase letter, figure, symbol)

"In addressing e-mails, @'s have become important." (symbol)

Plurals of academic degrees

Although traditionally academic degrees have used periods in their abbreviations (for example B.A., M.A., Ph.D.), the accepted practice now is definitely toward omitting the periods (for example, BA, MA, PhD—see page 139). I mention this here only because using periods or not using periods in the abbreviations of academic degrees can affect the way you form the plural of those abbreviations (see the procedures for forming the plurals of abbreviations discussed in the previous subsection). I recommend omitting these periods because that is the wave of the future. Here are some examples of correctly forming the plural of academic degrees that are abbreviated.

> "The faculty is comprised of people with PhD's in several different fields."

There are no interior periods, but there is a combination of capital and lowercase letters, which needs an apostrophe and an *s*. If you use the more traditional abbreviation with periods, the plural would be the same because of the combination of capital and lowercase letters.

> "The faculty is comprised of people with MAs and PhD's in many fields."

MA is made plural by adding only an *s* because there are no internal periods. PhD, on the other hand, is made plural by adding an apostrophe and an *s* because there is a combination of upper- and lowercase letters.

> "The graduation ceremony was for students earning MAs."

Abbreviations with more than one letter with no interior periods form the plural by adding only an *s*. The older format using periods would form the plural by adding an apostrophe and an *s* ("M.A.'s").

Plural of words used as nouns

Many times words that are not nouns are used as nouns. In the past, these words were made plural by adding an apostrophe and an *s* ('s). If you rely on your old high school or college English grammar book and it was published prior to about 1975, you will probably find the plural of such words formed in this way. But that is an outdated usage. Current usage calls for words that are not nouns but are used as nouns to form the plural by simply adding an *s* or *es* without any apostrophe. Here are some examples. You may be surprised at some of the correct usages.

"There are no ifs, ands, or buts about it."

"The dos and don'ts are clearly spelled out in the bylaws."

"Be sure to use your whiches and thats correctly."

"Threes and fours are a lot of fun."

"It is important to write your thank-yous promptly."

There are, however, some exceptions to this practice. For example, using "yesses" and "noes" is preferable, but using "yes's" and "no's" is still considered permissible usage, though somewhat behind the times. For clarity purposes, it is considered preferable to use "maybe's" instead of "maybes."

Plural nouns used as singular

The plural form of some nouns is singular in both meaning and use. Let's look at some examples.

"The good news is proclaimed by ministers and priests."

"Politics is a complicated subject."

"The headquarters is located in Chicago."

"Bad news is what seems to make the headlines."

Singular form wrongly used as plural

It is quite common for a singular noun to be wrongly referred to as a plural. This happens frequently when referring to a company, an organization, or a group. Here are some examples of *incorrect* usages of a singular noun being referred to as a plural.

> "I like doing business with ABC Company. They really manufacture good widgets."

ABC Company is singular, and "they" is plural. You should say, "The company manufactures good widgets," or "The employees manufacture good widgets." You definitely should not, however, use a plural pronoun (they) to refer to the singular ABC Company.

> "The business group meets every Wednesday morning over coffee. They discuss how to generate traffic in the downtown business district."

"Group" is singular, and "they" is plural. It is true that a group by its very definition is comprised of more than one person. But when referring to the entire group and not individual members of it, "group" is a singular noun, as is "committee," and should be treated as such. Group would only be used as a plural if you were referring to more than one group.

> "The high school civics class is learning community service. They are responsible for picking up trash on Main Street."

"Class" is singular, and the word "they" is plural. This is incorrect usage.

"ABC Company has a good mail-order department.
They are so efficient."

"Mail-order department" is singular, and "they" is plural. This just will not work!

Although referring to the singular form of a noun as a plural is common practice, it is incorrect. Be careful to use the singulars and plurals of nouns and pronouns as they are meant to be used.

Plural of italics

Names of newspapers, magazines, and journals and the titles of books are printed in italic type. When publications are used in the plural, the *s* added to the end of the publication's name to make it plural should not be in italic type, but in roman type (the primary or usually used type). The rationale for this is quite simple. The *s* added at the end is not part of the actual name of the publication; it is simply the letter used to indicate the plural of the publication's name. Only the actual name of the publication should be in italics.

Let's take a look at the following examples.

"He wanted to buy two *Chicago Tribune*s."

The name of the newspaper is the *Chicago Tribune*, and it should appear in italic type. The *s* tacked onto the end of "*Tribune*" is in roman type because it is not part of the actual name of the newspaper; it is used here simply as the sign of the plural.

"Several *Ladies' Home Journal*s were in the magazine rack."

The title of the periodical, *Ladies' Home Journal*, is in italic print, but the *s* tacked onto the end of "*Journal*" is used to indicate the plural, is not part of the title of the periodical, and is, therefore, in roman type instead of italic type.

When the actual name of the book or periodical ends in *s* and it is used in the plural form, unlike the general rule for making singular nouns that end in *s* plural by adding *es*, the title is left unchanged and is printed in italic type. Here are some examples.

> "There were *New York Times* spread all over his large desk."

Since the name of the newspaper ends in the letter *s*, it is used in the plural without following the general rule of tacking the sign of the plural onto the end of it.

> "The newsstand never seems to run short of *Washington Post*s, *Lebanon Daily Record*s, *Milwaukee Journal-Sentinel*s, and *Fallen Angels*."

The first three entries have the actual name of the newspaper in italics and the *s* that indicates the plural form of a singular noun in roman type. The last entry, which refers to the title of a book, is entirely in italic type because the name of the book is *Fallen Angels* (plural).

In dealing with the plurals of the names of publications, it may be more practical just to rearrange the sentences so the plurals are not needed. For example, going back to the previous four examples, let's reword them so the plurals are not necessary.

> "He wanted to buy two copies of the *Chicago Tribune*."

> "Several issues of the *Ladies' Home Journal* were in the magazine rack."

> "Several copies of the *New York Times* were spread all over his large desk."
>
> "The newsstand never seems to run short of a supply of the *Washington Post, Lebanon Daily Record, Milwaukee Journal-Sentinel*, and *Fallen Angels*."

This material dealing with plural forms of nouns should not be taken as an article in an encyclopedia and does not address *every* conceivable configuration and use of plural nouns. It does, however, cover the situations that most people will be confronted with. If you are faced with an unusual case of making a noun plural that is not discussed in this portion of the bonus section, you will need to reach for *The Chicago Manual of Style* or *Merriam-Webster's Collegiate Dictionary.*

Part C: Forming the Possessive Case: Irregular and Special Examples

The possessive case indicates ownership, belonging, possession, or relationship. This portion of the bonus section addresses irregular and special constructions for forming the possessive case of nouns and pronouns that are not addressed in chapter 6. But before turning to the more unusual noun possessives, let us restate the procedures for forming the great majority of noun possessives.

The general rule for forming the possessive case of nouns is as follows:

✓ The possessive case of most singular nouns is formed by adding an apostrophe and an *s* ('s).

✓ The possessive case of most plural nouns ending in *s* is formed by adding only an apostrophe (').

✓ The possessive case of most plural nouns *not* ending in *s* (usually referred to as irregular plurals) is formed by adding an apostrophe and an *s*.

✓ This general rule holds true with family names and letters used as a name.

Using the "of" construction

Before proceeding with examining the exceptions and special cases of forming the possessive case, let's take a look at what is generally referred to as the "of" construction of forming the possessive of nouns. The general rule for forming the possessive of nouns calls for the use of an apostrophe, either by itself or with an *s*. Sometimes it may be less awkward to use the "of" construction to indicate possession instead of adhering to the general rule. For example, instead of saying, "The house's roof leaks," it may seem more natural to say, "The roof of the house leaks"; or instead of "The car's driver was drunk," I would find it easier to say, "The driver of the car was drunk."

There is no hard-and-fast rule as to when the "of" construction should be used. There was a time when good standards of grammar called for the "of" construction to be used when the possessing noun (that is, the thing doing the possessing and not the thing being possessed) was an inanimate object and the general rule to be used when the possessing noun was a living, animate being. But those times have passed. This is one of those instances where grammatical practices have gone through a transitional period.

Mrs. Jones, referred to in the introduction, favored keeping the distinction between when to use the general rule and when to use the "of" construction in forming the plural of nouns. Having learned much of what I know about grammar from Mrs. Jones, I also favor keeping the distinction. I think it leads to greater clarity and just sounds better. But whether you use the "of" construction in this way is entirely up to you. Either way is correct when the possessing noun is an inanimate object. There is no choice, however, about using the general rule when the possessing noun is an animate being. When that is the case, the general rule or one of the exceptions noted in the following paragraphs should definitely be adhered to.

General rule for forming possessive case of pronouns

There are several exceptions to the standard practices of forming the possessive case of nouns that we will examine later. Before addressing them, however, let's turn our attention to understanding more thoroughly the possessive case for pronouns. This is important because sometimes forming the possessive of nouns and pronouns is closely related, and a general knowledge of both is helpful.

The general rule for forming the possessive case of pronouns is

✓ personal pronouns use no apostrophe to form the possessive case; and

✓ indefinite pronouns add an apostrophe and an *s* to form the possessive case.

The standard practices associated with using the general rule for forming the possessive case of pronouns were addressed in chapter 6. Let's delve into the complexities and intricacies of forming the possessive case of pronouns.

The seven possessing pronouns and their independent forms

There are seven possessive pronouns in the English language, and each of these pronouns has what is called an independent form. They are as follows:

Possessive pronouns	Independent forms
my	mine
our	ours
your	yours
his	his
her	hers
its	its
their	theirs

Using pronouns and their independent forms with nouns

The possessive pronoun must be used with a noun (my coat, our house, your books, his car, etc.). The independent form also may be used with a noun (the coat is mine, the house is ours, the books are yours, the car is his, etc.). But the independent form, unlike the possessive pronoun, may stand alone without a noun. It may, however, stand alone without a noun only if the noun, although not written or spoken, is clearly understood.

Using independent forms without nouns

Using the independent form of a possessive pronoun without a written or spoken noun—the noun being simply understood—is a construction that is used less frequently. In fact, people sometimes hesitate to use this construction because they wonder if it is grammatically correct. Using the independent form of a pronoun without a noun is grammatically correct, and here are some examples of how that works.

"Put your coats with theirs in the bedroom."

One understands that "theirs" refers to coats belonging to other people, although that is not actually said.

"We'll put ours on the bed with theirs."

Coats are never mentioned in this sentence. Yet we know that "ours" and "theirs" refer to coats. The independent forms of the possessive pronouns can stand alone, as they do in this sentence, when what they are referring to is clearly understood.

"Did you put mine with theirs in the bedroom?"

Again, coats are not mentioned, but they are understood because they have been referred to in previous sentences. Therefore, the independent forms of possessive pronouns are used.

"Will you bring me hers when you get mine from the bedroom?"

Coats are not mentioned, but are understood.

Independent form used as the subject

An independent form of a possessive pronoun may also stand alone and be used as the subject, as long as the subject of the sentence is understood, although not specifically mentioned. For example, "Hers is in the bedroom"; "His is still in the car"; and "Theirs are on the bed in the bedroom." Again, coats are not mentioned, but from the context of what has been said, we know that the subject of these examples is "coat" or "coats."

Cardinal rule: no apostrophes with possessive pronouns

In all of the above examples about the use of any form of the possessive pronoun, it is crucial to recognize that *no form of the possessive pronoun ever uses an apostrophe. That is a cardinal rule!* I know of no exceptions to this rule.

Compound personal pronouns

Several personal pronouns form compounds by adding "self" or "selves" to the end of the pronoun. For example: "my" becomes "myself"; "our" becomes "ourselves"; "your"—"yourself" or "yourselves"; "him"—"himself"; "her"—"herself"; "it"—"itself"; and "them"—"themselves." *These compound personal pronouns do not have possessive forms and cannot be used as possessives.*

Proper names to express possession

Proper names may also be used to express possession in the same ways that the independent forms of the possessive pronouns do. Referring to the "coats" of earlier examples, the following are sentences that use proper names to express possession, even when the noun (coat or coats) is not specifically mentioned, but is clearly understood.

> "Put your coats with Jim's and Nancy's in the bedroom."

> "We'll put ours on the bed with Bob's."

> "Who put Bob's with Jill's and Frank's in the bedroom?"

> "Will you bring me Jill's when you get mine from the bedroom?"

> "Frank's is in the bedroom."

> "Pete's is still in the car."

> "Jim's and Nancy's are on the bed in the bedroom."

Possessive of noun compounds

The generally accepted practice for forming the possessive of noun compounds is to add the appropriate ending to the final word of the compound. The initial words of the compound, whether singular or plural, will remain the same when converting the compound noun to the possessive case. It is only the last word of the multiword noun, whether the compound is formed with or without hyphens, that will indicate possession, and it is only the last word of the compound noun that will indicate whether the singular or plural form of the possessive case is to be used. That seems simple enough at first glance. But as one sorts though the following examples, it becomes a little tricky.

As pointed out in part B of the bonus section, which deals with forming the plural of nouns, the last word of a compound noun may be singular or plural, depending on whether the principal word of the compound is the first or the last word of the compound (see page 105). Since it is always the last word of a compound noun that indicates possession, one must pay attention to the specific singular, plural, and irregular qualities of the last word of the compound noun being converted to the possessive case. Remember, it is only the last word of the compound that changes.

All of the following examples represent *correct* constructions of forming the possessive case of multiword nouns or phrases.

> "Her mother-in-law's sisters..."

Possession of a compound noun always is indicated by placing the sign of the possessive case on the last word of the compound. In this example, the compound noun is "mother-in-law." The last word of the compound is "law." The possessive case of a singular noun is indicated by adding an apostrophe and an *s*. Change "law" to "law's." It makes no difference whether that which is being possessed (in this case "sisters") is singular or plural.

> "His father-in-law's friends..."

The last word of the compound is "law." The singular possessive case is indicated by adding an apostrophe and an *s*.

> "His parents-in-law's other children..."

Whether the principal word ("parents") is singular or plural makes no difference in forming the possessive case; the initial words of the compound remain unchanged when forming the possessive case. The possessive case of a compound noun always is formed by making the last word of the compound possessive. Add the sign of the possessive singular—an apostrophe and an *s*. Change "law" to "law's."

"The attorney general's daughter..."

The compound noun is made possessive by making "general"—the last word of the compound—possessive. Add an apostrophe and an *s*.

"The attorneys general's children..."

Two or more attorneys general, and two or more children. But the number of attorneys and the number of children are immaterial. The last word of the compound is what matters, and the last word of this compound is "general" (singular). Make this compound possessive by adding the singular form. Add an apostrophe and an *s* to "general."

"The King of England's wife..."

Last word of compound noun made possessive.

"The student assistant's friend..."

In this example, the principal word of the compound is the final word of the compound instead of the first ("student *assistant*"). That makes no difference. The possessive sign is added to the last word of the compound, regardless of whether the last word is or is not the principal word. Use the sign of the singular possessive. Add an apostrophe and an *s* to "assistant"—"assistant's."

"The student assistants' friends..."

Two or more student assistants and two or more friends. "Assistants" (plural) is the last word of the compound ("student assistants"). Make "assistants" possessive by adding only an apostrophe, the possessive sign for a plural noun ending in *s*. The number of friends makes no difference in making this determination.

"The chief executive officer's secretary..."

The sign of the possessive is added to the last word of the compound: "officer" (one officer); add an apostrophe and an *s*—"officer" becomes "officer's."

"The chief executive officers' association..."

In this example, "officers"—the last word of the compound—is plural (refers to several officers who are members of the association); add only an apostrophe, the possessive sign for a plural noun ending in *s*.

"John Jones Jr.'s father..."

The full given name—John Jones Jr.—is the compound noun. The last word of the compound is "Jr." The sign of the possessive is added to the last word of the compound. Hence, "Jr." becomes "Jr.'s." It is important to realize that the period after "Jr." is part of the given name. The sign of the possessive, the apostrophe and *s*, is added after the period in "Jr."

Possessive for companies, organizations, and so forth

The possessive forms used in names of companies, organizations, agencies, publications, and governments vary considerably. Some government, corporate, and institutional agencies and organizations use apostrophes in their names when possession is indicated. For example, People's Republic of China, National Governors'

Association, Actors' Equity Association, *Ladies' Home Journal*, Young Men's Christian Association, Young Women's Hebrew Association, and Lloyd's of London use the sign of the possessive. There are, however, many that do not use apostrophes, such as Citizens Advisory Committee, United Nations Day, Diners Club International, General Motors Corporation, Farmers Mutual Insurance Company, Municipal Taxpayers League, *Publishers Weekly*, and West Side Boys Club. And then there are those that use the "of" construction: Union of Soviet Socialist Republics, Department of Foreign Affairs, National Academy of Sciences, National Association of Stock Car Auto Racing, United Federation of Teachers, and Veterans of Foreign Wars.

Be sure to spell the names of the various agencies, organizations, companies, and the like as the agencies themselves do. That includes expressing the possessive case as they do. If you are uncertain about the exact spelling of any such names, turn to your dictionary, *The Chicago Manual of Style*, or to the websites of the respective agencies, organizations, companies, and so forth.

To form the possessive case of companies, organizations, agencies, and the like, follow the generally accepted practice for forming the possessive of multiword noun compounds: add the appropriate ending to the final word of the compound and keep the initial words of the compound unchanged. See the following examples.

"National Governors' Association's membership…"

The sign of the possessive is added to last word of the compound name. The last word of the compound name is "Association." "Association" becomes "Association's," possessive for singular possessing noun.

"Actors' Equity Association's customers…"

The same rationale used with the previous example applies here. The singular "Association" becomes possessive by adding an apostrophe and an *s*—"Association" becomes "Association's."

"Lloyd's of London's bookkeepers..."

"Lloyd's of London" is singular—one company. It makes no difference how many bookkeepers there are. Change the last name of the compound name to indicate singular possessive by adding an apostrophe and an *s*—"London" becomes "London's. However, this is a case of the possessing noun being an inanimate object (a company), and it may be less awkward to use the "of" construction: "The bookkeepers of Lloyd's of London."

"Citizens Advisory Committee's records..."

Use the general rule. Add the sign of the singular possessive. "Committee" becomes "Committee's."

"General Motors Corporation's vehicle inventory..."

"General Motors Corporation" is singular—one company. Change the last word of the compound name to indicate singular possessive by adding an apostrophe and an *s*—"Corporation" becomes "Corporation's." Again, you may find it a smoother construction to use the "of" construction: "the vehicle inventory of General Motors Corporation."

"Of" construction not used with plural place names

When the last element of the name of a place or organization is a plural form ending in *s*, the "of" construction is not used. In all such cases, the possessive case is formed by adding only an apostrophe. For example, United States' foreign policy, Forrest Hills' mayor, Wetland Gardens' maintenance director, and Honeybees' chief executive officer. In all of these cases, the last word of the entity's name is a plural form ending in *s*; hence, the possessive case is formed by adding only the apostrophe.

Possessive with italics

The names of newspapers, magazines, and journals and titles of books are printed in italic type, and, for the most part, they follow the general rules for making nouns possessive. But there are some nuances that need to be observed. Here's an example to show you what I mean.

> "The *Ladies' Home Journal*'s readers number into the thousands."

The last word of the compound name is "*Journal.*" You should make it possessive by following the general rule for making a singular noun possessive—add an apostrophe and an *s*. "*Journal*" becomes "*Journal's.*" But take a careful look at this example. Italic type is used because *Ladies' Home Journal* is the name of a magazine. But the apostrophe and the *s* tacked onto the end of "*Journal*" are not italicized because they are not part of the title of the magazine; they are merely the sign of the possessive and do not deserve to be in italic type. We looked at this same matter in part B of the bonus section, under the heading of "Plural of italics" (see page 110). I might also point out that this is another instance in which I recommend using the "of" construction. Although it is grammatically correct to use either the general rule or the "of" construction for forming the possessive in this sentence, I think it sounds better and makes a stronger sentence to say, "The readers of the *Ladies' Home Journal*..." instead of saying, "*Ladies' Home Journal's* readers..."

Joint possession and individual possession

If two or more nouns share ownership in or a relationship with the same thing or person, the possessive form is added only to the last noun. If two or more nouns do not share in the ownership or relationship of a thing or person, the appropriate possessive form is added to all the nouns. See the following examples and their explanations.

"Let's meet at Nancy and Bill's house."

Both Nancy and Bill share in the ownership of the house; the sign of the singular possessive (apostrophe and *s*) is added only to "Bill"—the last name.

"Nancy's and Bill's cars are in the garage."

Nancy has a car, and Bill has a car. The cars are owned separately; each name takes the singular possessive sign.

"Nancy's and Bill's fathers enjoy playing golf."

Nancy and Bill have separate fathers; the sign of the singular possessive is added to each name.

"Nancy and Bill's children enjoy playing golf."

Nancy and Bill are the parents of the same children. This is a joint relationship; singular possessive sign is added only to the last name—to "Bill."

"James, Anderson & Peters' Hardware always has ample inventory."

The hardware company is owned jointly by all three people. The sign of the possessive is used only on the last word— "Peters."

"Minneapolis and St. Paul's transportation system serves the two cities well."

Joint ownership of the one transportation system that serves the Twin Cities means the sign of the singular possessive is added only to the last name, "St. Paul."

"Chicago's and New York's transportation systems experience heavy use."

Each city has its own transportation system. The sign of the singular possessive is added to both "Chicago" and "New York."

Possessive of nouns plural in form and singular in meaning

As noted in part B of the bonus section, some plural nouns are singular in meaning and use (see page 108). For example, "news," "politics," "economics," "headquarters," and "mathematics." Nouns plural in form but singular in meaning always *form the possessive case by only adding an apostrophe*—the sign of the possessive case called for by the general rule as it relates to plural nouns ending in *s*. The "of" construction should not be used with these nouns. The following are correct examples for the possessive case of nouns plural in form but singular in meaning. The pertinent words are in italic type for easy identification.

"The *news'* impact on the public is very significant."

"Political science majors interpret *politics'* impact on world affairs."

"*Economics'* main thrust is the study of the production, distribution, and consumption of goods and services."

"The *headquarters'* staff works very long hours."

"*Mathematics'* impact on scientific professions is generally considered to be greater than its impact on the more artistic professions."

Possessive forms of diseases

Some diseases are plural in form, but are used in the singular sense: for example, "measles" and "mumps." The same general rule is followed in making them possessive as is used for other nouns that are plural in form but are used in the singular sense—add only an apostrophe after the s (*measles'* or *mumps'*).

It has become common practice for the names of some diseases to be shortened and transposed to the possessive case. Although one would seldom find that kind of usage among trained medical personnel or in medical literature, most authorities on grammar agree that in general literature such a practice is quite acceptable. For example, Down syndrome becomes "Down's," Alzheimer's disease becomes "Alzheimer's," and Hodgkin's disease or Hodgkin's lymphoma becomes "Hodgkin's." When what you are writing calls for the possessive form of a disease to be used, it will behoove you to do some research on the subject. *Merriam-Webster's Collegiate Dictionary* is a good place to start. If you become a serious writer or editor of medical literature, specialized stylistic guides should be consulted. See, for example, *American Medical Association Manual of Style* or *Scientific Style and Format*.

Possessive nouns that are the same in singular and plural

As noted in part B of the bonus section, the plural and singular of some nouns are spelled the same, for example, "Burmese," "Chinese," "Japanese," "chassis," "corps," "sheep," "moose," and "swine" (see page 104). In forming the possessive of such nouns, treat them all as plurals, even if the meaning is singular. That means, for nouns that have the same singular and plural form ending in s, form the possessive case by adding only an apostrophe; those nouns *not* ending in s form the possessive case by adding an apostrophe and an s. See the following examples:

Spelling the same, singular or plural	Possessive form, singular or plural
Burmese	Burmese's
chassis	chassis'
corps	corps'
quail	quail's
swine	swine's

Possessive forms of holidays

Names of holidays showing possession are inconsistent. The names of a number of American holidays form the possessive case by adhering to the general rule for nouns. For example, Mother's Day, Father's Day, New Year's Day, Valentine's Day, St. Patrick's Day, and April Fool's Day—all singular—show possession by adding an apostrophe and an *s*. Parents' Day and Presidents' Day—both plural—also follow the general rule and form the possessive by adding only an apostrophe. But there are those holidays that show no signs of possession: Martin Luther King Day, United Nations Day, and Veterans Day. And that reminds one that Daylight Saving Time is neither possessive nor plural.

Most people give little thought to the possessive signs used with holidays. Most good dictionaries will have major holidays listed, and that's a good place to check the exact spelling of holidays.

Part D: Principal Parts of Verbs Made Easy

As pointed out in chapter 7, the principal parts of a verb are (1) the present tense, (2) the past tense, and (3) the past participle. We habitually use verbs without thinking very much about them. Only occasionally do we have to stop and think about whether or not the form of the verb we are using is correct. We have become accustomed to hearing what is right and wrong, and we speak or write accordingly. But popular usage has sometimes caused us to hear the wrong thing, and we have responded by developing bad grammatical practices. This is the case with both regular and irregular verbs—with verbs that we use frequently and those that we use occasionally.

No one is expected to memorize and remember the spelling of the principal parts of all the verbs that are used most frequently, much less those that are used only now and then. There are literally thousands of them. I have found it very helpful to have a "cheat sheet" always close at hand, providing an easy reference for the verbs that many of us seem to have the most trouble with.

Part D of the bonus section is meant to be just that kind of a ready reference. It includes the three principal parts of an extensive list of verbs—both regular and irregular—that we use on a rather regular basis and some that we use only occasionally. Part D does *not*, however, include *all* the verbs in the English language. Such an undertaking would be a book in itself. It does include the verbs that, in the experience of this writer, will meet the needs of the average person. If the verb you are looking for is not included here, I suggest you utilize a recent edition of *Merriam-Webster's Collegiate Dictionary*.

The verbs are listed in alphabetical order. With most verbs, there is no question about the exact spelling of each of the three principal parts. But with the principal parts of some verbs, there are variant spellings. When that is the case, all variant words are included.

In some cases where variants are listed, there is absolutely no preference as to which of the forms should be used—the variants are considered equally correct, and it is a matter of personal choice as to which should be used. In those instances the variant words are separated by "or."

In some cases, however, one variant is more popular and is considered preferable to the other(s). When this is the case, the word(s) considered less preferable is placed in parentheses. If you want to use the word in parentheses, it is certainly permissible. You just need to know that the less preferable form of the verb, although currently correct, is probably in a transitional phase and will, in time, be considered either incorrect or on equal standing with the other variant.

There are a few principal parts of verbs included in part D that are considered incorrect by general standards of spelling and grammar but are used regularly and are considered proper in particular regions or areas of the country. Such words, representing a particular regional dialect, are enclosed in brackets. Unless you are writing solely for a particular region or what you are writing is intended to be representative of a specific area, colloquialisms should, in my opinion, be avoided. It is a very questionable practice to attempt to use colloquialisms if you are not from, or very well acquainted with, the area the colloquialism is used in.

Occasionally a note of explanation or clarification will accompany a verb in the following list of verbs and their principal parts.

Principal Parts

Present Tense	Past Tense	Past Participle
am	was	been
arise	arose	arisen
argue	argued	argued
attack	attacked	attacked
awake	awoke (awaked)	awoken or awaked (awoke)
bear	bore	borne (born)
beat	beat	beaten
become	became	become
begin	began	begun
bend	bent	bent
bet	bet (betted)	bet (betted)
bid	bade or bid	bidden or bid (bade)
bite	bit	bitten or bit
bleed	bled	bled

Present Tense	Past Tense	Past Participle
blow	blew	blown
break	broke	broken
bring	brought	brought
broadcast	broadcast—broadcasted, common form among radio broadcasters	broadcast—broadcasted, common form among radio broadcasters
build	built	built
burn	burned or burnt	burned or burnt
burst	burst (bursted)	burst (bursted)
bust	busted (bust)	busted (bust)
buy	bought	bought
calm	calmed	calmed
catch	caught	caught
choose	chose	chosen
climb	climbed	climbed
cling	clung	clung
come	came	come
cost	cost	cost
creep	crept	crept
cut	cut	cut
deal	dealt	dealt
dig	dug	dug
dive	dived or dove	dived (dove)
do	did	done
drag	dragged	dragged
draw	drew	drawn

Present Tense	Past Tense	Past Participle
dream	dreamed or dreamt	dreamed or dreamt
drink	drank	drunk or drank
drive	drove	driven
drown	drowned	drowned
drug	drugged	drugged
dwell	dwelled or dwelt	dwelled or dwelt
eat	ate	eaten
fall	fell	fallen
feed	fed	fed
feel	felt	felt
fight	fought	fought
find	found	found
flee	fled	fled
fling	flung	flung
flow	flowed	flowed
fly	flew—in baseball, "flied out"	flown—in baseball, "flied out"
forbid	forbade (forbad)	forbidden
forget	forgot	forgotten or forgot
forgive	forgave	forgiven
freeze	froze	frozen
get	got	got or gotten
give	gave	given
go	went	gone
grow	grew	grown
hang	hung (hanged)	hung (hanged)
hang—to execute	hanged (hung)	hanged (hung)

William B. Bradshaw, PhD

Present Tense	Past Tense	Past Participle
have	had	had
hear	heard	heard
hide	hid	hidden
hit	hit	hit
hold	held	held
hurt	hurt	hurt
keep	kept	kept
kneel	knelt or kneeled	knelt or kneeled
know	knew	known
lay	laid	laid
lead	led	led
lean	leaned [leant]	leaned [leant]
leave	left	left
lend	lent	lent
let	let	let
lie—to recline	lay	lain
lie—to be untruthful	lied	lied
light—to set fire to, to brighten or illuminate, to settle on or alight, to fight (light into)	lit or lighted—"lighted" common when meaning "to set fire to," especially in the Midwest; popular trend for all usage in all areas of the country appears to be moving toward "lit," but either is considered correct	lit or lighted

Present Tense	Past Tense	Past Participle
loose—to unfasten or relax	loosed	loosed
lose—to mislay or to suffer defeat	lost	lost
make	made	made
mean	meant	meant
meet	met	met
mistake	mistook	mistaken
pay	paid	paid
prove	proved	proved or proven
put	put	put
quiet	quieted	quieted
quit	quit (quitted)	quit (quitted)
read	read	read (all principal parts spelled the same, but past tense and past participle pronounced differently from present tense)
ride	rode [rid]	ridden [rid or rode]
ring	rang	rung
rise	rose	risen
run	ran [run]	run
say	said	said
see	saw	seen
seek	sought	sought
sell	sold	sold

Present Tense	Past Tense	Past Participle
send	sent	sent
set	set	set
sew	sewed	sewed or sewn
shake	shook	shaken
shine—to glow	shined or shone	shined or shone
shine—to polish	shined	shined
shoot	shot	shot
show	showed	showed or shown
shrink	shrank or shrunk	shrunk or shrunken
shred	shredded	shredded
shut	shut	shut
sing	sang or sung	sung
sink	sank or sunk	sunk
sit	sat	sat
sleep	slept	slept
slide	slid	slid
smite	smote	smitten or smote
sow	sowed	sowed or sown
speak	spoke	spoken
spend	spent	spent
spin	spun	spun
spit	spit or spat	spit or spat
split	split	split
spread	spread	spread
spring	sprang or sprung	sprung
stand	stood	stood
steal	stole	stolen

Present Tense	Past Tense	Past Participle
stick	stuck	stuck
sting	stung	stung
stink	stank or stunk	stunk
strike	struck	struck (stricken)
strive	strove or strived	striven or strived
swear	swore	sworn
sweat	sweat or sweated	sweat or sweated
sweep	swept	swept
swim	swam	swum
swing	swung	swung
take	took	taken
teach	taught	taught
tear—to shed tears	teared	teared
tear—to damage	tore	torn
tell	told	told
think	thought	thought
thrive	thrived or throve	thrived (thriven)
throw	threw	thrown
tread	trod (treaded)	trodden or trod
understand	understood	understood
wake	woke (waked)	woken or waked (woke)
wear	wore	worn
weave	wove or weaved	woven or weaved
weep	wept	wept
win	won	won
write	wrote	written (writ) [wrote]

Appendix

Keeping Up-To-Date: Ten Short Reminders

During our years of elementary and secondary education, we learn the basics of English grammar. But it is not enough to rely on what we have learned in the past. It is necessary to stay up-to-date in English grammar, just as it is in any field. However slowly, standard practices of grammar *do* change, and it is not always easy to keep up-to-date on the changes.

I have included in this appendix ten short reminders of changes in grammar that have taken place over the last twenty-five to thirty years, changes that may be different from what you learned in high school or college. Scholars have been debating some of these changes for 475 years, and some scholars are still debating them. Their views tend to be influenced by their respective scholarly specialties, that is, whether they majored in ancient, medieval, or modern English literature or grammar. But the issues discussed in the appendix have been agreed upon by the majority of today's scholars, with the exception of a few die-hards who have clung to their outdated views.

Although they are not among the big ten of grammar, the changes discussed in the appendix are changes that we need to be aware of.

"Can" and "may"

My personal experience and observation in the classroom have led me to conclude that the great majority of grammar instructors teach that "can" should be used to express one's *ability* to do something and "may" to express one's *permission* to do something. But, contrary to what many classroom instructors believe and teach, "can" has been used both to ask for and grant permission since the 1800s and is considered entirely appropriate by most of today's scholarly resources for English grammar, especially in daily speech. Although I personally favor using "may" to grant permission, using "can" is considered grammatically correct. For formal writing, however, I still strongly recommend using "can" and "may" in the more traditional ways.

Ending sentences with a preposition

The notion that it is improper to end a sentence with a preposition is a concept of yesteryear—a superstition with no historical basis. There is no question about it: it is permissible to end a sentence, either spoken or written, with a preposition. It is up to the personal preference of the speaker or writer. To illustrate, in each of the following examples which of the two sentences sounds better to you: "Whom is she going to the movie with" or "With whom is she going to the movie"; or "There are many rules of grammar I need to be aware of" or "There are many rules of grammar of which I need to be aware"; or "Whom am I speaking with" or "With whom am I speaking"? They are all correct. Take your pick!

Starting sentences with a conjunction

There is absolutely no historical or grammatical foundation for suggesting that it is incorrect to start a sentence with a conjunction. This is another groundless superstition. As *The Chicago Manual of Style* puts it, quoting Charles Allen Lloyd: "One cannot help wondering whether those who teach such a monstrous doctrine ever read any English themselves" (page 258, 16th edition).

Starting sentences with conjunctions—"and," "so," or "but"—has long been practiced in classical and formal writing of the highest caliber. It is perfectly all right to start a sentence with a conjunction. In fact, sometimes it seems more logical and preferable in drawing conclusions and making transitions to begin a sentence with a conjunction.

No periods after academic degrees

In the past, it was the accepted practice to use periods in the abbreviations of academic degrees and professional certifications, for example, B.A, M.A., M.B.A., LL.D., M.D., Ph.D., Ed.D, C.P.A, and R.N. Over the years, however, this has been changing, and now most recognized authorities on grammar, including *The Chicago Manual of Style* and *Merriam-Webster's Collegiate Dictionary*, recommend omitting periods in such abbreviations. For example, the accepted practice for making such abbreviations is now: BA, MA, MBA, LLD, MD, PhD, EdD, CPA, and RN. These are meant only as examples of some of the most used degrees and certifications; not including periods applies to the abbreviations of all academic degrees and professional certifications. For forming the plural of such abbreviations, review pages 106-107 in the "Bonus Section."

Spelling out of numbers

The spelling out of numbers has definitely changed in recent years. It used to be that the accepted standards of grammar called for numbers from one through ten to be spelled out and above ten to use numerals. Now, except in technical and scientific contexts, the following uses are recommended:

• Whole numbers from one through one hundred are spelled out, using hyphens to combine numbers, and most numbers above one hundred use numerals (for example, "Forty-one children from eleven churches were riding in the five vans" and "The two parking lots provide spaces for 144 cars").

• Round numbers (hundreds, thousands, hundred thousands, and millions) are spelled out and hyphens are not used with them (for example, "About four hundred people lived in the small community, but they were near a city of two hundred thousand people and lived in a state with a population of more than five million people").

• All numbers used to begin a sentence are spelled out (for example, "Nineteen fifty-three was an unusually hot year" and "One hundred fourteen children attended camp"). If a year alone is used, it is expressed in numerals unless it stands at the beginning of a sentence (for example, "We know that 1953 was an unusually hot year").

• These procedures apply to cardinal numbers, what we think of as regular numbers ("one," "two," "three," "four," etc.) and to ordinals, numbers ending in "st" or "nd" or "th" ("first" or "1st," "second" or "2nd," "third" or "3rd," "fourth" or "4th," etc.). Here are some examples: "The eleventh person to apply was awarded the 109th position out of the 410 positions available" or "She placed second and her good friend came in near the end in 141st place." It should be noted that when specific dates are expressed, cardinal numbers are used, although these may be pronounced as ordinals. For example, "October 27, 1932, has special significance for me."

• Centuries are spelled out and not capitalized.

Using "ly" after spelled-out numbers

I was taught in college to use "firstly," "secondly," "thirdly," and so forth, when introducing sections or segments of written reports, pamphlets, leaflet, or articles. That may have been correct grammar then, but it certainly is not now. Although the use of "firstly," and the like, can be traced back to about 1532, I know of no creditable grammarian today who suggests that usage. You should simply say or write "first," "second," "third," and so on.

"Further" and "farther"

For many, many years "farther" and "further" were used interchangeably. But in the late 1940s they began to take on slightly different meanings, and today they definitely are used with different meanings.

"Farther" is now used to indicate distance: for example, "Bill ran farther than Joe," or "Chicago is farther from St. Louis than Kansas City is." "Further" is now used to indicate time, degree, or quantity: for example, "I need to look into the matter further before making a decision" or "My research needs to go further before I write the report."

Using simple personal pronoun

It is appropriate to use a compound pronoun for emphasis. For example, "She saw the president himself " or "I will fix that myself" or "The queen herself mingled among the commoners." But in the 1940s, people began to practice a much broader use of the compound pronoun, and today, in my opinion, it borders on being out of hand.

The following examples of using the compound pronoun (instead of the simple personal pronoun) are becoming more and more popular, and they are incorrect: "The committee gave the report to myself" or "Bill and myself are going to Reno together" or "They brought the stuff to Ellen and myself." Be correct; just keep it simple: "The committee brought the report to me" or "Bill and I are going to Reno together" or "They brought the stuff to Ellen and me."

There is a prevalent theory among scholars that the practice of using the compound pronoun came about because people were not certain whether they should use "I" or "me," so they began to use "myself." If you are in question about the correct use of "I" and "me," you should probably review the first chapter of this book.

William B. Bradshaw, PhD

"Sure" and "certain"

"Sure" and "certain" are both used to express lack of doubt about something. But they are used differently, depending on how one reached the conclusion that there is "no doubt." "Sure" is used to express one's belief of "lack of doubt" through intuition or feeling: for example, "I am sure she loves me" or "I am sure I did well on the exam" or "I am sure we will get the apartment we want" or "I am sure I forgot to turn off the iron." "Certain," on the other hand, is used when one reaches the conclusion of "absence of doubt" based on facts, evidence, or definite grounds of some kind, rather than feeling: for example, "After looking at the report, I am certain the company did the right thing" or "Based on my research, I am certain that my position is the correct one" or "The police are certain that the evidence confirms his guilt."

"Good" and "Well"

Scholars have argued about the proper uses of "good" and "well" for more than two centuries, especially where the two words are used in connection with the senses—sight, hearing, smell, taste, and touch. Regardless of what you have heard, read, or been taught, the prevailing position among English grammar scholars today is that either "good" or "well" can be used in connection with the senses, depending on which of the two words sounds or looks better to the one speaking or writing.

I personally prefer "good" in referring to taste, touch, and smell: for example, "The food tastes good"; "The sand feels good to my feet"; and "The perfume smells good." I go back and forth between "good" and "well" with the other senses depending on the context of the sentence: for example, "The doctor tells me I hear well for my age"; "Good hearing is important for one's safety"; "I see well"; and "I am grateful for good sight."

The accepted practices of grammar, however, have changed when using "good" or "well" to express one's condition of health.

It used to be that it was only considered correct to say, "I feel well." But currently, nearly all reliable scholars agree that either "well" or "good" can be used after "feel" in describing one's health: "I feel good" and "I feel well" are both correct. Take your pick!